Endof

In *Fire on the Family Altar*, Cheryl Sacks releases a clarion call to experience the power of Holy Spirit in our homes. Establishing an altar for fresh fire today is not about building a physical structure or maintaining a natural fire. Rather, the altar God desires is a heart and home where worship originates. Our Holy God wants an altar, a place of pure and wholehearted relationship, where He can meet with us and His fire can be seen in us. Without a daily place, an altar where the fire within can be stoked hot, we walk common to the world around us. Cheryl is a general of prayer, and what she shares could not be more timely for inviting Holy Spirit to be at home in us. Allow this incredible handbook to shift the atmosphere of your home and ignite the fire of His passion in the next generation.

DR. CHUCK D. PIERCE
President of Glory of Zion International, Kingdom Harvest Alliance,
and Global Spheres Inc.

It is my prayer that every believer will read Cheryl Sacks' book, *Fire on the Family Altar*! God gave her a vision that I pray resonates with every follower of Jesus. God said to her: "Revival will come to America when the *family altar* is restored!" This exploded in my heart and mind. I grew up in the generations when most believers had family altars, and families who prayed together, stayed together. In my family, those who wandered away returned and God was glorified! The foundation of past generations is the family altar!

If you do not have a family altar in your home, now is the time to begin. Cheryl shares amazing experiences and gives spiritual inspiration and guidance to help you begin and maintain the family altar in your home, in your church, and your community. Prayer precedes national revival! Let's do this and proclaim America shall be saved!

GERMAINE COPELAND
Author of the Prayers That Avail Much Series
Founder of the Prayers That Avail Much Ministries (aka Word Ministries, Inc.)

There are a handful of prayer leaders I know personally who have mastered the art of intercession and have a history of direct cause-and-effect answers to prayer. Cheryl Sacks is at the top of my list. She has a perspective on family and family living that should be classified as "expert advice." In her new book, Cheryl shows us how to transform families, beginning by igniting the fire of the Holy Spirit in our own home. Having engaged in the seven mountains of culture from a biblical worldview for decades, I believe that the family mountain, hands down, is the most important!! That's why I highly recommend Cheryl's latest book *Fire on the Family Altar*.

DR. LANCE WALLNAU
CEO, Lance Learning Group

In just two generations our culture has essentially destroyed the institution of family, leading to untold pain, devastation, and despair. Now, best-selling author Cheryl Sacks has written a thorough and practical guide for families about how to prioritize relationship with God and prayer in their homes. *Fire on the Family Altar* provides a clear road map families can use to lead a desperately needed return to God that will spark the greatest awakening yet!

LEN MUNSIL, B.S., J.D.
President, Arizona Christian University

There has never been a greater battle for the family than right now. In this book, my friend Cheryl Sacks imparts a crucial message that will ignite faith and Spirit-inspired strategies for believers in this hour. Can our nation be truly saved and transformed? I believe the answer is a resounding yes—one family at a time.

DR. CHÉ AHN
Senior Pastor, Harvest Rock Church, Pasadena, California
President, Harvest International Ministry
International Chancellor, Wagner University

I fully believe that *Fire on the Family Altar: Experience the Holy Spirit's Power in Your Home* is a must read for every Christian home. This Holy Spirit-inspired message is a now word for the season of revival and awakening we are in. Cheryl beautifully shares great wisdom, revelation, and biblical truths along with prayers and action steps to activate a move of God, revival, and the manifest presence of His glory within your family and home. As families and homes become a habitation of His glory, awakening will sweep this nation. Thank you, Cheryl, for this timely word.

REBECCA GREENWOOD
Cofounder, Christian Harvest International and
Strategic Prayer Apostolic Network

Families today need spiritual help, and *Fire on the Family Altar* can give it to them! I've known Cheryl Sacks for years and can attest that she knows families, she knows prayer, and she knows the power of the Holy Spirit! You will get all of that knowledge through the practical and inspiring pages of *Fire on the Family Altar*. Let it change your family!

JONATHAN GRAF
Publisher, *Prayer Connect* magazine
President, Church Prayer Leaders Network

The battle in our culture today is clearly over the family. Satan hates strong marriages and healthy parent/child relationships. Broken families tear down society, but fortified families can transform a nation. *Fire on the Family Altar* will equip you to transform your own family through reviving the family altar, empowering you to rebuild the ruins of our broken world.

JANE HAMON
Apostle, Vision Church @ Christian International
Author: *Dreams & Visions, The Deborah Company, Discernment and Declarations for Breakthrough*

This is the best book I have ever read on prayer and the family! As a dad and husband for many years, I can confidently say this book has the power to change the culture of your family forever! It is full of simple and practical tips to help you establish an atmosphere of God's presence in your home! I truly believe that revival and awakening will come as the family altar of prayer is restored in our homes.

DR. JASON HUBBARD
Executive Director, International Prayer Connect

Genesis 1 starts with God restoring order to a world in chaos. And after God rearranged everything in the earth back into divine order, His answer to keeping this order in the earth was a family! The family was God's plan for restoring the Kingdom of Heaven again on earth. This is why the family has been under unprecedented attack since the Garden and is experiencing an all-out assault in this generation. Satan knows that in order to destroy the earth, he has to destroy the family. But whenever there is a yoke, God raises up an anointing to destroy it. In her book *Fire on the Family Altar*, Cheryl Sacks is once again reviving this mandate to the family and in the earth! This is indeed a book whose time has come!

ISAAC PITRE
President, Isaac Pitre Ministries
Founder and Overseer of Christ Nations Church
Leader of II Kings Global Network
Dallas, Texas

FIRE
ON THE
FAMILY ALTAR

Experience the Holy Spirit's
Power in Your Home

CHERYL SACKS

CONTRIBUTING WRITER
HAL H. SACKS, DMIN

DESINY IMAGE® PUBLISHERS, INC.
P.O. Box 310, Shippensburg, PA 17257-0310
"Promoting Inspired Lives."

This book and all other Destiny Image and Destiny Image Fiction books are available at Christian bookstores and distributors worldwide.

For more information on foreign distributors, call 717-532-3040.
Reach us on the Internet: www.destinyimage.com.

ISBN 13 TP: 978-0-7684-6424-5
ISBN 13 eBook: 978-0-7684-6425-2
ISBN 13 HC: 978-0-7684-6427-6
ISBN 13 LP: 978-0-7684-6426-9

For Worldwide Distribution, Printed in the U.S.A.
1 2 3 4 5 6 7 8 / 27 26 25 24 23

DEDICATION

To my beautiful grandchildren
Luca, Rocco, and Cosetta Reginelli

CONTENTS

FOREWORD

By Dutch Sheets

I've traveled several million miles throughout America, encouraging and teaching the Body of Christ regarding prayer. Sometimes I jokingly say I'm like Johnny Cash, "I've been everywhere, man, I've been everywhere." On this journey, I've had the privilege of meeting many wonderful people, including thousands of committed intercessors and hundreds of faithful leaders. As skilled and mature as these esteemed warriors and generals truly are, I can say with complete confidence—none are better at what they do than Cheryl Sacks and her amazing husband, Hal.

Cheryl and Hal coordinate prayer for the entire state of Arizona, blanketing it with mature intercession. Pastors trust them, educators love them, business leaders seek and respect their counsel, and intercessors follow them to war. They are well known in both Heaven and hell. Just for the record—even at the risk of sounding like Captain Obvious—Cheryl Sacks is uniquely qualified to write this book!

Now let me state something that may not be quite as obvious: This is *not* a book about family devotions. It is a collection of tested insights that will help you bring the fire and presence of God into your home, family, and life. Far from being a religious instruction manual, it is a guide to spiritual success, victory, and prosperity for you and yours.

In Scripture, altars were built to welcome the fire of God, which then prepared the way for the presence of God. Religious routines, even important disciplines, can become stale, boring, and lifeless if not energized by the presence and power of Holy Spirit. The apostle Paul warned us that we can have forms or rituals that appear godly, but are not infused with the power of Holy Spirit (see 2 Tim. 3:5). Attend a prayer meeting or conference led by Cheryl Sacks, however, and you'll quickly realize she is all about the presence and power of Holy Spirit. Her books carry the same dynamic. This is why two of the sections in this book are titled "Encountering the Lord Alone and with Others" and "Shifting the Spiritual Climate—Drawing the Presence of God."

Another of the *many* things that sets this book apart is its practicality. While powerful and revelatory, it is also extremely practical. This has always been one of Cheryl's and Hal's greatest strengths. They not only *share* truth, they also teach us how to *apply* it. This book is one of the best marriages of revelation and wisdom, impartation and application that I know of. So often, we're told what but not how. You will *not* experience that frustration after finishing this book. You'll be able to *do* the teaching!

It is great to read about fire falling on Elijah's altar and glory filling Solomon's Temple; it's exciting to hear about power from Heaven and tongues of fire on the disciples in the Upper Room; but these accounts are merely theology until the fire, glory, and power make their way to our house. That is what *Fire on the Family Altar* is all about.

Dutch Sheets
CEO/President, Dutch Sheets Ministries
Publisher of the daily devotional Give Him 15

FOREWORD

By Cindy Jacobs

The first institution that God created was the family. It is the building block of society. So, it makes sense that satan would attack it fiercely. One only needs to look around and see the effect of broken homes on our generations.

Therefore, this is not only an important book but a critical one. Cheryl Sacks has identified a major stronghold that is right in front of our faces—the destruction of the family. But God has a plan. It is His heart to bring revival to the nation through families praying and worshiping together.

Sounds simple, right? Not simple—it is profound. There is nothing more bonding, more healing, than a family on their knees together and talking to God.

Cheryl has done us all a huge favor in writing this book. She gives examples of the healings and miracles that have taken place when families pray together and invite God's glorious presence into their homes. Reading *Fire on the Family Altar* reminded me of how my preacher daddy would have us all kneel beside the bed and pray each night before we went to sleep. I will never forget the sound of his deep, baritone voice crying out to God for each of us and our destinies. From that rich foundation, the Lord grew those prayer seeds until one day I would build worldwide intercessory movements. This is one of the most powerful things that happens at the family altar—we can pray for our children to fulfill their God-given calling and destiny.

Since Cheryl and I have been friends for 30 years, I have watched how time and time again she has prayed and received answers from God. For this reason, I highly recommend the prayers in the Appendix that you can personalize for your own life and family, such as "Praying Breakthrough for a Troubled Marriage," "Praying for Your Children's Schools," "Your Family's Future and Calling," and "Praying for Loved Ones to Know Christ." In fact, this powerful material is worth the price of the book alone!

Fire on the Family Altar is a practical book. It will help you activate your family's prayer life. It will show you how to change the spiritual atmosphere in your home and experience the Holy Spirit's power. There is something in it for singles as well as family units. Read this book carefully and put the revelation it contains into use. It will heal your family, the family of God, and your nation!

CINDY JACOBS
Cofounder, Generals International

PART ONE

THE PURPOSE AND POWER OF A PRAYER ALTAR—THEN AND NOW

CHAPTER 1

THE VISION: LIGHTING THE NATION

Arise, shine, for your light has come, and the glory of the Lord rises upon you. See, darkness covers the earth and thick darkness is over the peoples, but the Lord rises upon you and his glory appears over you. Nations will come to your light, and kings to the brightness of your dawn (Isaiah 60:1-3 NIV).

I will never forget the moment. I was on stage at a large church conference, about to lead prayer for revival in America. As I stood quietly, the Holy Spirit suddenly spoke to me in a resounding, almost audible voice.

I nearly fell over! His words rang out with a force and urgency that shocked me:

"REVIVAL WILL COME TO AMERICA WHEN THE FAMILY ALTAR IS RESTORED!"

This came entirely out of the blue. No one at the conference was talking about the family. It wasn't even remotely what I expected to hear from the Lord.

As these words reverberated through me, I couldn't help but think of all the cultural depravity and complex problems facing America. *How could something as simple as families praying, reading the Bible, and worshiping together bring spiritual life to an entire nation?*

"Your plan sounds rather...*simplistic*," I replied to the Lord.

No sooner had I said this than a young man walked onto the platform and began to pray the exact words I'd just heard: *"Lord, restore the family altar in homes across America!"*

Wow! What a confirmation!

At that moment the heavens seemed to open before me, and I saw a vision of the nation covered in deep, impenetrable darkness. Suddenly, as I looked closer, I saw a few homes begin to light up, glowing like stars across the dark night sky. The fireplaces in these homes were burning brightly where families were sitting together passionately praying and praising the Lord. Then, all at once, homes everywhere across the nation exploded with light as the families inside were worshiping and praying. This spread like wildfire until the whole nation was ablaze with the power and presence of God.

I could only stand in awe—what I saw took my breath away!

"Lord," I cried out, "Could it really be? Is *family* the very key to unlocking the revival we've been praying for?"

THE COMING MOVE OF GOD'S SPIRIT

In the days that followed, the Lord began to speak to me that He is coming to visit households not only across America, but around the world. The Lord showed me that as families worship Him and invite His Holy Spirit into their homes, He will revive them—bring them back to life. His presence and power will fill their lives and households, igniting a passion and hunger for God that will spread to those around them.

This would not be the first time God has used the family altar to spark a revival. In the late 1600s, a Puritan minister named Thomas Boston was burdened by the state of his church in Scotland, which was not only spiritually cold but practically empty. He began visiting in the homes of his members and asking them specifically about their spiritual needs. Boston discovered that some of his people were not even sure they were saved, and he led many to Christ. In each home he read the Bible and prayed and challenged the head of the house to begin a family altar each day. In a matter of months, a revival broke out in their community that filled the church and changed the people's lives forever. It all started with a family altar.[1]

In the times in which we are living, God is calling His people to once again light the family altar—to establish our homes as places to regularly meet with and encounter Him. He is saying, "I want to come into your home in a fresh, new way!" I believe as God's people respond to this invitation, it will usher in an unprecedented move of the Holy Spirit, filling households with healing, restoration, and a renewed love for God and one another. In fact, in my vision the Lord showed me "fire from Heaven" falling on families, spreading to the family of God—a concentric move of God that starts in our own hearts as the Holy Spirit prepares us to once again become a place where He is welcome.

The fire of God is coming to *purge* sin—everything that separates us from God and one another. He will ignite righteousness and passion for the Kingdom! This will awaken the nation spiritually like nothing before it, lighting a fire that burns deep in the hearts of families and throughout the family of God.

The Holy Spirit will bring a deep work as believers repent of their wrong attitudes toward God and one another. This will provoke tangible demonstrations of love, unity, and honor among God's people. Offenses will be laid down as believers repent of jealousy, unforgiveness, bitterness, and competition. This holy fire will burn up everything that had been built on a foundation of wood, hay, and stubble, so that our lives and homes are built on a firm foundation (see Rom. 14:10-12; 1 Cor. 3:11-15).

It is interesting to note that one definition of *revival* is "to return to its original intent, condition, or purpose." That is what the Lord will do in this next great move of the Holy Spirit. He will restore our homes and fill them with His presence—the same way that the first family, Adam and Eve, lived and communed with God in their garden home.

I know you may feel, as many people do, that your life, family, nation, or "_____" (fill in the blank) is too broken to be restored. But this simply is not true! The Bible speaks of this hope through the many stories of broken lives and a nation (Israel) seemingly too far from God to be restored. Yet, when His people called to Him, seeking Him with all their hearts, the Lord always answered. He restored.

This is not the time to give up on your spouse, child, or grandchild. God hasn't given up on our families, so why should we? This is not the time to give up on your nation. This is the time to cry out to God, to make your home an altar of prayer and worship to Him, and watch how He releases His power from Heaven to earth.

GET READY!

There are things the Lord wants to say to us and our families during these extraordinary times. I hear the Lord's urgent call to His Church, "Get ready, get your houses in order, and make room for My Spirit to move with power!" This is a clarion call for us to get into position for an outpouring of His Holy Spirit that will fill and overflow our homes, bringing in a great harvest of souls.

I feel a strong, weighty urgency of the Lord to draw near to Him—to get off the proverbial hamster wheel of our everyday lives, to get quiet long enough to hear His voice and be willing to do what He's asking of us. If we are running ahead too quickly and not listening to the Lord's voice, if we are holding too tightly to "what was" or what is comfortable, we will miss what the Lord is saying and what He is wanting to do in and through our households. We must pay attention!

I feel this is what the Lord is asking of all of us: "Are you willing to make the changes needed? To change and shift as I lead? To speed up when I say, 'Go quickly'? Will you welcome Me to make the changes when I say, 'Behold, I am doing a new thing'? Will you slow down and wait patiently when I impress upon you, 'Be still and know that I am God'?"

We all must be willing to change, to allow Him to put things in right order—to give our families a divine *reset.*

YOUR HOME CAN BE A STOREHOUSE OF HIS GLORY

It is possible to make your home a storehouse of God's glory, presence, and provision in times of cultural crisis. You also may desire to connect with other praying families as "houses of prayer" to erect a canopy of God's presence. You and those around you can create communities of refuge, much like the land of Goshen was for the Jewish people in Egypt. For the Israelites, Goshen was a place of God's special protection and provision. God told His children, *"You shall dwell in the land of Goshen, and you shall be near me, you and your children and your children's children, and your flocks, your herds, and all that you have"* (Gen. 45:10 ESV). Goshen became a flourishing place of refuge in the time of God's judgment when the angel of death passed through the nation—and they were spared (see Exod. 12).

This is not a call for the Church to hide in our homes; it is a time for the Church to arise and shine, as the prophet Isaiah proclaimed: *"Arise, shine, for your light has come, and the glory of the Lord has risen upon you"* (Isa. 60:1 ESV). The Lord is signaling that there is coming a fiery move of His Spirit *within* homes that will bring rapid revival and a move of His Spirit in communities, cities, and nations.

The days we are living in are filled with tremendous stress, and the Scripture tells us this will only increase (see 2 Tim. 3:1). People will be looking for those who know how to touch God on their behalf. As the revival spreads, many new believers will need more of God's Good News—the "basics" of the Bible. This is why the Lord is calling us to prepare our homes to be a habitation for Him, filled with His presence, so that it is a warm and inviting place to disciple the harvest.

In this next season, as followers of Christ, we are going to need each other as never before. The enemy of our faith will push back against this move of God with all his might and power. The Lord is calling us to reach out to friends and neighbors—to invite them into our homes for times of Spirit-filled worship, prayer, and sharing

God's faithfulness in our lives. Even as we see in the Acts of the Apostles when the early Christians were persecuted for their faith, they met together daily in homes, sharing meals and drawing courage by praying and worshiping together (see Acts 2:42-47). They left these times of encounter with the Lord empowered to preach the Gospel boldly (even with the threat of imprisonment or death), heal the sick, and raise the dead.

Just as we saw in the early Church, the gift of hospitality will be a vital component of this next great move of God.

> *The end of all things is near. Therefore be alert and of sober mind so that you may pray. Above all, love each other deeply, because love covers over a multitude of sins. Offer hospitality to one another without grumbling. Each of you should use whatever gift you have received to serve others* (1 Peter 4:7-10 NIV).

Nothing is more effective at drawing people into the Kingdom and discipling them than nurturing friendships in a warm home setting. A friend of mine, Merrily, and her husband, Paul, regularly invite friends to their home for meals and to do life together. Sometimes these are friends from church or parents of their kids' friends from school, soccer, or gymnastics—most of whom are not yet believers in Christ.

Merrily had been talking about the Lord with her personal trainer, Jen, and with the children's babysitter, Christina. So, when Merrily and Paul planned a night of worship with extended family and friends, they decided to invite Jen and Christina.

Several guests brought instruments—a keyboard and guitars— and everyone joined in worshiping the Lord. It wasn't a formal program, but rather just a casual time of friends getting together to focus on Jesus.

Jen, who had never been inside a church, said later that her experience was so profound that she could barely stand; she felt "like Jell-o." She thought she might at any moment burst into tears. At the time, Jen was separated from her husband and was ready to file for divorce. But as a result of that encounter, Jen came to faith in Christ. She began to pray for her husband and her marriage. Shortly after that her husband reached out to her asking if they could talk. He agreed to go to counseling and the two of them reconciled.

Christina also encountered the Lord that night and began asking Merrily a lot of questions. She wanted to know more about God and what a personal relationship with Him looked like. At the time, Christina was under a lot of stress at school, and her relationship with her boyfriend, Josh, was stuck in an unhealthy cycle, filled with arguing and fighting.

One morning at two o'clock, Christina called Merrily, crying. Christina and Josh had been out late drinking, and Josh had gotten in a fight with another family member. When Christina tried to step in and stop them, she inadvertently got struck in the face and there was blood everywhere.

Merrily drove to pick up Christina. She brought her back home, cleaned her up, and put her to bed in the guest bedroom. The following morning, they prayed together. That same week, Paul reached out to Josh, and over the next few months began to meet with him regularly for prayer and Bible study.

The troubled couple started going to church with Merrily and Paul. They accepted Christ and were water baptized and filled with the Holy Spirit. They put their relationship under the lordship of

Jesus Christ and were married. Today, Christina and Josh are one of the happiest couples you will ever meet. They beam with love for each other and the Lord. And they've expressed they want to do for others what Merrily and Paul did for them.

These are the same kinds of encounters the Lord wants all of us to experience regularly in our homes. He wants to be the center of our marriages and families. He wants His Holy Spirit to be like a fire burning in our homes, so that everyone who walks through our front door will encounter His tangible presence.

As our families become saturated with God's heart and filled with His hope, joy, and love, we will reignite in others that which was reignited in us.

Whatever the season of life you and your family are in, there is an urgency in this hour for us to prepare our hearts and homes for this extraordinary move of God. I hear the Lord's urgent call, even a promise, to our families and to the family of God today: *"If you will build an altar, I will come—with awakening and revival fire— to your family and to your nation!"*

ACTIVATION: DEDICATING YOUR HOUSE TO THE LORD

The practice of dedicating a home to the Lord has been common since Old Testament times. We are not only dedicating the house to God for His purposes—the walls, doors, rooms, and objects— we are dedicating all the activities within it. Joshua said before the people of Israel: *"As for me and my house, we will serve the Lord"* (Josh. 24:15 NKJV). We can make this same declaration.

Ideally you will do this with your spouse and children, but you can do this alone if they are not quite ready. You also may want to invite friends from your Christian community to join you. You don't need a priest or pastor to dedicate your home, but they would be a wonderful addition if you'd like to invite them.

1. Gather your family in one central location, such as your living room, and pray a prayer of dedication for your home. The prayer can be as simple as this: "Lord, we dedicate this house to You for Your purposes. Surround and fill our home with Your love, and may it be used to show Your love to all who enter here. Help us to reflect You in our hospitality. May we seek, honor, and encounter You here every day."

2. Pray for God's protection over your home. You might say something like this: "Lord, we ask You to protect our home from all evil. Watch over every member of our household and over all our possessions. We ask You to send Your angelic hosts to surround our home and to put a barrier around every gateway into our home."

3. Then go through all the rooms of your house and pray an individual blessing in each room, using anointing oil, if you like. Anointing oil may be purchased at a Christian bookstore or website, or you can simply use olive or cooking oil. You may want to anoint (put a smudge) on all the gateways into your home, such as doors, windows, fences between you and neighbors, the TV, and internet lines. If you live near the water, be sure to include praying over the dock as well.

4. You may like to ask God to give you a special Scripture to pray over your home. If your children participate, they can choose a special Scripture to pray over their own room.

5. Record the Scripture and date by writing it on a doorframe, under a threshold, on a plaque, in a family Bible, or some other place of significance.

LET'S PRAY

Dear Lord, our families and nation need You as never before. Only You can bring the healing and reconciliation we so desperately need. I ask You to send a sweeping nationwide revival and let it begin in my home.

I know that as my family and other families invite Your holy presence and power into our homes, we will see a massive returning to You, Your Word, and Your ways. I decree, in Jesus' name, that the family altar is being restored, and a movement of family prayer and worship is being ignited to set the nation ablaze with the power and presence of Almighty God! Amen!

CHAPTER 2

WHAT IS AN ALTAR?: WHY YOUR FAMILY NEEDS ONE

Remember, the fire must be kept burning on the altar at all times. It must never go out (Leviticus 6:13 NLT).

You might be new to the concept of a "family altar." Maybe you're asking, "Just what is a prayer altar? Why would my family need one?"

When we talk about building an altar today, it does not mean erecting a physical stone altar, the way God's people in the Old Testament did. As a believer in Christ Jesus, the altar is your heart, and the fire that's ignited inside you is the presence and power of God.

When we speak of a "family altar," we are talking about establishing times when we come together to meet with God and invite His Holy Spirit into our home in a way that changes the atmosphere. The family becomes more God-centered, and His presence begins to affect our relationships and the activities that take place in our home.

Everything important in the life of a child of God happens at an altar because the altar is the place where you have intimate conversations and grow in relationship with the Lord. It's the place where Heaven touches earth—where your heart responds to His presence and His heart responds to your needs and longings.

God's blessing and provision are secured at an altar. Salvation is found at the altar. God's healing power is released at an altar. Everything you need is obtained in that place of close communion and exchange with the Lord. If you need an answer or direction from God, it can be found as you draw near to Him at the altar. If you are seeking deliverance from a spirit of oppression or the dark cloud of depression, your deliverance can be found at an altar! Everything that requires God's supernatural intervention for your breakthrough is obtained in that meeting place with Him.

Do you want God to change things in your home, your family, or your children's lives? (If you are like most people I know, your answer is a resounding "YES,"—that's likely the reason you are reading this book.) Let me encourage you that your miracle is found at the altar.

Do you want to see revival in your city? It starts at an altar. God is going to demonstrate His power to you and your family as you encounter Him at the altar!

Altars have always been places of communication and exchange between God's people and their Maker. In the Old Testament, Israel built these earth, wood, and stone structures to offer animal sacrifices for their forgiveness and to honor, worship, and meet with their God (see Gen. 8:20; Judg. 6:22-24). Every time God's people dedicated an altar to the Lord, a tangible transaction occurred between Heaven and earth.

WHAT DOES IT LOOK LIKE?

The family altar is different for every family and even in different cultures across the world. However, every family altar has similar components: reading the Word, ministering to the Lord in worship, and prayer.

Many families spend significant time together at the altar, often for an hour once a week, some every day, and others two or three times during the week. No matter how frequent, the main idea is to establish an atmosphere where the Holy Spirit is touching every area of life in the home. God's presence is affecting conversations and attitudes, helping resolve conflicts, and changing the way family members relate to one another. This fresh, life-giving atmosphere is transforming the family's values, mindsets, and how they spend their time.

The Holy Spirit's presence can be seen affecting other people as they visit the home, whether they are extended family members or friends. The entire family begins to see the presence of God changing the way they live, talk, and think.

BEFORE YOU CAN EXPERIENCE THE FIRE OF GOD, YOU NEED TO REBUILD THE ALTAR OF GOD

As you pray for the fire of God—His presence and power—to fall upon your home and nation, it's essential to understand this principle: unless there is an altar, there can be no fire! The prophet Elijah knew this—he called for God's people to come together, and *"he repaired the altar of the Lord that had been torn down"* (1 Kings

18:30 TLB). Elijah knew that before he could see the fire of God, he needed to rebuild the altar of worship to God.

Today, the Lord is calling our families to return to their righteous inheritance so that the fire of God's goodness will light up our homes, communities, and nation. The first step toward national revival is to restore the family altar and prepare our homes for the fire of God to fall.

Most people in our nation do not know what a "family altar" is or its importance. Families gathering in their homes, praying together, and worshiping the Lord were commonplace in the formation of America. Early pioneering families started and ended their days with family prayer, especially at mealtime. Likewise, families praying and reading the Bible together every night was a practice that continued into the mid-20th century and marked the First and Second Great Awakenings.

During the '60s, however, prayer was pushed out of public schools and the civic arena. Even in churches, the prayer altars vanished, and family prayer in homes disappeared. Today, most families in the U.S. have no idea of or interest in family prayer, and in most cases, family members are too distracted to pray together. The family altar of worship and prayer has fallen into disrepair.

EXAMPLES OF GODLY ALTARS IN THE BIBLE

The saints of old built altars for many reasons, but they were always the location of an exchange between Heaven and earth. We can learn much by looking at these meeting places with God that apply to us today:

- Noah built an altar to thank the Lord after He spared his family from the flood. God found it pleasing, and responded to Noah's action with a promise that He would never again destroy all living things with a flood (see Gen. 8:20-21).

- Abraham built an altar in the place where God made an everlasting covenant with him, giving him the land of promise for his family and descendants forever (see Gen. 12:7).

- Jacob, after wrestling with the Lord, realized the goodness of God and called for his household to cleanse themselves of all their foreign gods. The next day he built an altar to the God of his fathers, commemorating that place where he had experienced this life-changing encounter (see Gen. 35:1-7).

- Joshua built an altar to honor and celebrate God's faithfulness, His covenant, and for bringing Israel into their promised land, giving them a great military victory (see Josh. 8:30-34).

- Gideon tore down two pagan altars of idolatry and rebuilt them to the living God when he answered God's call to deliver Israel from the Midianites. And the God of Peace, El Shalom, was once again established (see Judg. 6:11-29).

- Elijah challenged the prophets of Baal around an altar, demonstrating the power of Yahweh over other gods (see 1 Kings 18:20-39).

In these instances and more, altars marked intersections where two kingdoms met, and transactions between people and their God occurred. The altars served as places of worship, sacrifice, communication, and covenant making. In some cases, these men of the Bible were both purging the land of evil and reclaiming it for Yahweh. Godly men and women passionately contended with the spiritual darkness that occupied their land as they called to God and invited His mighty presence to dwell there, overtaking the darkness evil brings.

In other cases, they were marking the place of their personal encounter with God or remembering a great deed He had done for them. In every case, every one of these altars acted as touchpoints, a spiritual "gateway" between Heaven and earth. When such heavenly thresholds were opened through sacrifice and worship, God personally revealed Himself in powerful ways, tangibly transforming and blessing those who met Him there. God still speaks to and blesses His people in that place of communion with Him today. He will do the same for you and your family when you spend time together with Him too.

THE FAMILY ALTAR TODAY

Don't let the idea of building a family altar intimidate you. It can start in a simple way. When your family gathers and prays around the dinner table, that's an altar. When you meet with God in your easy chair in front of a sunny window each morning, coffee in hand, that's an altar. When you pray with your children at night as you tuck them into bed or as you are driving them to soccer practice, those are altars too.

When God spoke to my friend Teresa about building a "family altar," she wasn't even sure what that meant. She certainly didn't know how to go about starting this in her home:

> One day as I was praying, I heard the Lord say, "Teresa, I want you to build a family altar."
>
> "What does that mean, Lord?" I asked. I sensed He was asking me to start a regular time of prayer and worship with my family. But how would this be possible since our two sons were grown and married, with children of their own? How were my husband and I to build a family altar if our children had already left the house? I told the Lord I was willing but needed a plan. As I waited, a simple idea dropped into my heart. I called the entire family and suggested that we fast and pray together every Tuesday. We all would miss breakfast and lunch and then gather at our home for dinner. Everyone agreed to try this.
>
> After the meal, we worshiped the Lord and prayed together. To guide our prayer time, I asked each of them a single question, "What do you want God to do for you in the coming week?"
>
> My daughter-in-law is a women's physician. She said she wanted to see healings and miracles in her practice, so we all prayed in agreement with her for that. Within a couple of weeks, the Lord began to answer! Since starting our weekly family prayer altar, my daughter-in-law has seen patients healed of tumors, women who could not previously conceive get pregnant, and many young women freed from depression and other serious problems.

Soon we couldn't wait until the next week to hear what God had done in everyone's life and how He was answering our prayers![1]

You might be asking why one simple pursuit and act of obedience produced so many miracles. Everyone in Teresa's family knew the Lord and was already praying on their own. So why the sudden results of answered prayer and miracles? I believe it is because they heard the Lord, obeyed Him, and built a family altar! By gathering the family for an intentional time of weekly prayer, combined with a half-day fast, they experienced breakthroughs they could have never expected.

Of course, it is absolutely powerful whenever *anyone* prays! The Bible tells us, *"The earnest prayer of a righteous man has great power and wonderful results"* (James 5:16 TLB). However, as Teresa's family learned, exponential power is released when we pray together, not to mention the very presence of God Himself! Notice the condition to having access to His power through praying *together* when Jesus said: *"Again I say to you, if two of you agree on earth about anything they ask, it will be done for them by my Father in heaven. For where two or three are gathered in my name, there am I among them"* (Matt. 18:19-20 ESV).

That's why the deceiver, satan, fights so hard to prevent our families from praying together—he knows the increased, multiplied power of God that is released when we do!

BENEFITS OF A FAMILY ALTAR

When you and your family pray, worship, and seek the presence of the Lord together, you will experience your Heavenly Father's profound love for you and find your capacity to love unconditionally will grow too. You will discover the shared joy of celebrating God and all He is doing in your lives. As you spend time together in His presence and invite His Holy Spirit into your home, you will see a wonderful transformation that:

1. Strengthens Family Ties

Our simple, honest, and transparent prayers are the pathway to developing intimacy with our Heavenly Father—as are our heartfelt and caring words toward one another. There is both a vertical and horizontal component of bonding, and both need to be in place for God's power to flow to us and through us. As our hearts become vulnerable and tender in our prayers toward God and one another, we become empowered to nurture deeper and more authentic relationships (see Eph. 4:32).

2. Resolves Conflict

When you pray with your family members (about tensions in the relationships), the Lord helps each family member see their part in the problem. Their eyes are opened to what they themselves can do to bring resolution. Praying and worshiping together draws God's presence, softens hearts, and sheds fresh perspective on the problems. When you humbly pray with your family, esteeming them higher than yourself, and ask the Lord to forgive you and remove the obstacles that divide relationships, you will see impossible situations change (see Phil. 2:3-5).

3. Changes Hearts

We often see into a family member's heart more clearly than anyone else does. We are given a couple options to handle what we see. One less productive way is to try to help that person by confronting them with their problem. That typically does not work! Often, the more successful way is to pray fervently, asking God to give you an overwhelming love for that person's need or situation while asking Him for the wisdom to know what to say, when to say it, or not to say it at all. All the while, keep asking God to bring His healing to your loved one's heart.

4. Creates Life-Giving Communication

When your family members take time to share their hearts with each other, it helps everyone feel valued. Coming together in His love offers a set-aside time to find out what is happening in each other's lives, discover one another's needs and dreams, and gives an opportunity to show we care about each other. So, consider taking the time to hear from each other before launching into prayer. It's good to start by asking questions to break the ice and get communication started; some examples of what you may ask someone might be:

- What is your most pressing challenge right now?
- What are you thankful for today?
- Is there anything you are hurt or disappointed over?
- What do you need God to do for you this week? (If anyone needs prayer for physical healing, see "Praying for Healing" in the Appendix.)

You also may begin your time together by sharing stories of miracles and answers to prayer (long ago or current). This creates an atmosphere of faith, hope, and encouragement. It is a way we can pass down the testimonies of God's goodness and greatness to our children and our children's children. (See "What Is Your Story?" in the Appendix for more guidance.)

5. *Encourages Reconciliation*

Our friend Nate Dorn, a father of five, says the first thing his family does in their prayer time is clear the air of any resentment they may be harboring toward one another; the family altar is a safe place for reconciliation. He says:

> You figure out really fast as a father that you cannot lead prayer with your family when things are not right between you and your kids, or between you and your wife. You don't do this when you have just come down too hard on one of your children, or when you've snapped at your wife at the dinner table, or in anger put her down in front of the kids. My wife cannot come to the prayer time and sit across from me with unresolved hurt or anger. Your children will see through this, so it takes humility. More than once my wife and I have needed to apologize to each other or to the kids before we begin our time of family prayer.
>
> The kids have learned to do this as well. We reconcile before we pray together. Nightly family prayer gives us a time, place, and format to acknowledge and ask forgiveness for ways in which we have hurt each other. This clears the air of tension, melts away bitterness, heals hearts, and restores an atmosphere of love and unity.[2]

For those of you who are living alone or who are without a natural family due to loss, have had a broken marriage, have never been married, or other circumstances, I want to say that it is appropriate to consider your spiritual family as family. God gives us spiritual fathers, mothers, brothers, and sisters; for many of you, they truly are your family. You can establish a prayer altar with them.

When I was in my twenties, and before I married, I met for prayer every morning with my roommate, a woman who attended my church. We knelt in front of the picture window in our apartment and prayed for the upcoming day, for our future mates, that God would use us to lead others to Christ. Soon we were seeing God-encounters at work and school, and scores of other young singles were flooding our apartment for prayer and Bible study.

FAMILIES PRAYING TOGETHER: A POWERFUL FORCE

An altar today means we build into our lifestyle the priority of praying, talking with the Lord, and drawing near to Him. We do this personally, together with our families, and in ever-increasing circles that include our churches, schools, workplaces, communities, and even nation.

Uganda, for example, is a nation previously devastated by war, dictators, and AIDS. Today Uganda is known for revival, unity, and miracles. Ugandan Christians are effectively establishing family prayer altars, and now this model is being adopted by believers in other nations. They, too, are seeing a transforming revival.

In his book *Prayer Altars,* Mark Daniel writes about visitors from Uganda who were guests in his home. He began to realize, from their example and eye-opening testimonies, the power of the family altar:

I remember when the Ugandans first came to the United States and began telling us that we needed to have family altars. To our embarrassment, every one of us confessed that we did not have one.

The Ugandans looked at us in shock; they knew we were leaving our families unprotected, allowing the forces of darkness to dominate the mindsets, attitudes, and atmosphere of our homes.

This had never occurred to us. We had just been fooled into going along with the customs of our day and time, thinking that we were too busy...but as we began to establish prayer altars, I was amazed at how much God began to change things in our homes.[3]

Daniel shared that as the American families who met the Ugandans were faithful to meet together at home with the Lord, they experienced a fresh hunger for the Lord:

There were so many things in our homes that we had been unaware of: unloving attitudes, harsh words, sarcasm, manipulative behavior, and selfishness; but as we established prayer altars, the atmosphere became more honoring, respectful, and godly...and our homes became quieter, more peaceful, and more loving.

After we started the prayer altars, our children began to come and confess things instead of hiding them, and we saw changes in our children that could only have been provoked by the Lord.[4]

Imagine what would happen if families regularly invited God's presence into their homes. What would God do if we prayed not only for one another but also for our schools, workplaces, and churches? What would God do if every time our families gathered, we asked Him to send another Great Awakening to our land?

I believe we would see our families filled with great joy as healing fills our homes, prodigals return, and revival breaks out like fresh fire upon the altar. We would see multitudes of people—a veritable harvest of souls—coming into God's Kingdom.

When we invite the presence of God into our homes around the family altar, God changes everything!

ACTIVATION: PRAYING FOR PREPARED HEARTS

1. Take some time to dedicate yourself afresh to pray with and for your family. Ask the Lord to guide you to think about how to create a regular time of prayer and worship. What would that look like in your home, for your family? (See "A Sample Family Altar" in the Appendix for more guidance.)

2. Before you approach your family members with the idea, pray about it. Ask the Lord to forgive you and your family for ways you've neglected spending time with and honoring Him. You may even want to set aside a time to fast and pray.

3. Pray for each family member, that God will begin to prepare their heart, that He will give them the desire

to come together and worship Him and to establish a "family altar" in your home.

4. Even if you feel some family members will not want to come to the altar, don't let that stop you. The time of worshiping and honoring the Lord does not just impact those sitting in the room while it is going on. Because the presence of God is being drawn into the house, the atmosphere is changing, so even if other family members are not participating, the Holy Spirit in your home will minister to them, working on their hearts and stirring their spirits.

LET'S PRAY

Heavenly Father, I am so sorry for my busyness and distractions and for neglecting to spend time with You, both personally and together with my family. Forgive me for not inviting You into every situation in our family. Nothing is too hard for You! I do not accept that "this is just the way things are." You are the God who turns around the impossible. Nothing is impossible for You!

Lord, right now, I dedicate my family to You, I commit to praying for them every day, and I purpose to look for opportunities for my family to pray together. I commit to make room for You in my life and my home so that You can do great things in and through us. Father God, please give my family a "reset" to help us make You the center of our thoughts, words, and activities. Empower us, by Your Spirit, to find time and ways to pray together that honor You and each other. I decree that my home is being filled with Your tangible presence and every family member is being transformed into the likeness of Jesus Christ. Amen.

CHAPTER 3

WHY SATAN OPPOSES THE FAMILY: IT'S ALL-OUT WAR!

Be sober-minded; be watchful. Your adversary the devil prowls around like a roaring lion, seeking someone to devour (1 Peter 5:8 ESV).

The first institution God established on earth was the family. It is, without question, the most important to God and the most hated by satan.

God's greatest desire and plan for us and our families is that we would live in peace and harmony with Him and each other—that we would enjoy walking together daily in His presence. He blessed us with the plentiful earth to watch over and govern. However, satan, God's sworn enemy, is hell-bent on destroying our families. We are in a battle of the ages. What is at stake is nothing less than the destinies of our children and grandchildren and the kind of world they will grow up in.

Evil forces on every side are attempting to pull families apart beyond anything we could have previously thought possible.

Hordes of demonic spirits have been assigned to use every deception and temptation imaginable to break up marriages and terminate the rights (and even the inclination) of parents to raise their children with a biblical worldview.

Ungodly influences are redefining and distorting God's original design for the family, right down to what it means to be a man or woman, boy or girl.

In one way or another, we all are experiencing the fallout of this battle in our personal lives: broken families (our own or those around us), unprecedented levels of anxiety and conflict, and the tragic collapse of the ideals that built our nation.

Is it any wonder then that we are currently seeing levels of brokenness and disintegration in families like never seen before? Know this: the battle is bigger than you even know. It goes beyond simply the stability and security and happiness of your family or mine. The very structure of the family unit is under attack, and thus the future of civilization is at risk. We are in a war over our families, and it's a battle of life and death.

AS THE FAMILY GOES, SO GOES THE NATION

Satan knows the value of family—how it was designed to be the bedrock of society, the basic building block of nations, and the future of God's work on earth. To the degree that families are strong, a nation is strong. To the degree that families fail, nations crumble. Satan knows that if he can destroy the family, he can destroy the nation. It is no wonder he has put a bull's-eye on the nuclear family. It is no wonder families everywhere are experiencing what feels like an all-out attack!

Perhaps you've never thought about how everything in the world revolves around the family:

The family establishes the values that influence all of society.

It is in the home that children learn right from wrong. The family is the place where character is formed in children—the place where they learn to honor God or deny Him. Thus, the effects of the family reach beyond the four walls of the home and extend to the moral, social, and civil life of the nation. Every young person steps from the door of home into the field of life. And the way our young people learn to conduct themselves at home is the same way they will conduct themselves in culture, transforming it for better or worse.

Family is the building block of a healthy economy.

Strong families produce wealth. For millennia, families have worked to create their own businesses, developing the flow of revenue. Even the root word for *economy* in Greek is *oikonomia,* which means "family" or "household management." Today, family-owned businesses are still the backbone of the economy in many nations. Thus, if we have stronger families, we have stronger schools, stronger churches, and stronger communities with less poverty and crime.

The Kingdom of God grows through families.

Much of the Bible is the record of how God worked through families to achieve His purposes: Moses and Aaron; Joseph and his brothers; Ruth and Boaz; Esther and Mordecai—and, in the New Testament, through families like Timothy, Lois, and Eunice; and Priscilla and Aquila. The covenants God made with Abraham, Isaac, Jacob, and later David all happened within the context of families.

The family is the foundation of salvation.

In fact, the apostles' explicit intention was to influence the family unit as a whole, as we see when Paul and Silas encountered the Philippian jailer:

> *Then he brought them out and asked, "Sirs, what must I do to be saved?" They replied, "Believe in the Lord Jesus and you will be saved, you and your household." Then Paul and Silas spoke the word of the Lord to him and to everyone in his house. ...And without delay, he and all his household were baptized* (Acts 16:30-33 BSB).

Over and over in the book of Acts, we see that entire households accepted the Gospel and were baptized together.[1] This is how the early Church grew so rapidly.

The family is the means by which the stories of God's goodness and faithfulness are passed down from generation to generation:

> *We will tell the next generation the praiseworthy deeds of the Lord, his power, and the wonders he has done...so the next generation would know them, even the children yet to be born.... Then they would put their trust in God and would not forget his deeds* (Psalm 78:4, 6-7 NIV).

Family is the blueprint for how God's Kingdom is established and grows on earth.

We see this when God gave a mandate for families in Genesis 1:27-28: *"be fruitful, multiply, and fill the earth"* (AMP). Satan hates the fact that humans are made in the image of the eternal God and that they can procreate and raise godly children to influence culture and rule the earth.

This last point leads to the most important aspect of why satan opposes the family. To understand the depth of the evil one's hatred for God's design, we must go back to creation and God's original blueprint.

GOD'S ORIGINAL DESIGN FOR THE FAMILY

The first family's home was set in the context of a beautiful garden. God's original design was that home would be like Heaven, saturated with peace and joy. Truly, it was Heaven on earth. Life for Adam and Eve was simple, and the highlight of their day was spending time with Him and each other. They filled their days walking and talking with the Lord, caring for the garden, and keeping it fruitful and protected. The Garden of Eden was a picture of God's design for home. His tangible presence was there. Adam and Eve had everything they needed in abundance.

We see this plan unfold when God created Adam and Eve and commissioned them as a family. Their purpose was to bring children into their world, raise them to walk with God, fill the earth, and inhabit it, expanding their garden home. As they did what God had instructed them to do, they would extend the rule of God's government throughout the earth.

We see God's plan for family clearly defined in the Genesis account:

So God created man in His own image, in the image
and likeness of God He created him; male and female
He created them. And God blessed them [granting
them certain authority] and said to them, "Be fruitful,
multiply, and fill the earth, and subjugate it [putting it
under your power]; and rule over (dominate) the fish of
the sea, the birds of the air, and every living thing that
moves upon the earth" (Genesis 1:27-28 AMP).

God established a partnership with Adam and Eve and empowered them to be fruitful, multiply, and take dominion in the earth.

You may be asking the question, "What did God mean when
He said to take 'dominion'?" In Hebrew, the word is *ra'dah,* which
means "to operate in authority, rule, tread down" and "conquer."
The Lord told Adam and Eve, "You will govern, manage, be fruitful,
multiply, and rule the earth with Me." The two Hebrew words used
for *fruitful* and *multiply* are *pa'ra* and *ra'ba. Pa'ra* means to bear fruit
like a tree, being productive and reproductive, while *ra'ba* means to
become great or many, to multiply and increase.

Also, the Hebrew word for *dominion* in verse 28 is *ka'bash,*
which signifies the need to subdue and dominate. God's original
intent was that His creation would be governed by humans.

Think about it—one of the primary themes of the Bible is,
"Who will rule the earth?" In its first chapter, God gets right to
the point: "I want family, and My family will 'rule' the earth (their
home) for Me (see Gen. 1:26-28). They will be the extension and
expression of My Kingdom's government there. This is how I will
release My influence, My righteous Kingdom ideals and ways, into
the whole earth." That is true, and it is profound.

The Hebrew word for *dominion* and *rule* in this Genesis passage makes clear that the Creator was delegating to Adam and Eve this responsibility (*ra'dah*)—"to rule over, to govern." The ancient Hebrew psalmist knew this truth when he changed the word *ra'dah* ("dominion" and "rule") in Genesis 1:28 to *ma'shal* in Psalm 8:6, which means "absolute dominion and rule through God." The psalmist clarified that God meant that all creation was delegated to Adam and Eve—"to rule over, subdue, and govern."

When God created Adam and Eve, male and female, in His own image, He gave them authority over everything He had made. Satan at this time was subject to Adam and Eve's authority! But, through deception, satan, coming as a serpent, convinced Adam and Eve to agree with and submit to his words in disobedience to God. In so doing, Adam and Eve forfeited God's goodness and relinquished their authority. They surrendered to satan the keys over mankind and the earth, submitting to his rule.

But that wasn't the end of the story—all was not lost. God knew this would happen and had created another plan; He had a "second Adam" ready to step in and redeem all mankind. So God sent into the world His one and only Son, Jesus, who was all man and sinless, to reclaim His creation and restore its governing authority (see Luke 10:19; 1 Cor. 15:21-25; Eph. 1:20-21; 2 Pet. 1:3). This unfolding story in the Bible narrates the clash of two kingdoms, God's and satan's, with mankind as the prize.

The history of mankind is all about whose family will rule the earth—God's or satan's. So, that is the heart of the matter. God designed family to carry out His purposes—to govern, manage, and rule, and to defeat satan's rule and reign in the earth. No wonder satan is doing everything in his power to dismantle the family and destroy our children's lives and future!

SATAN'S STRATEGY TO DESTROY THE FAMILY

Have you ever thought about this? Everything we see in the news headlines today, the most pressing assaults against our culture, are all aimed at the family. Every critical issue—marriage, sexuality, our children's identity, and the lives of babies in the womb—are at the epicenter of every battle:

- Divorce is attacking marriage as it ends it—breaking covenant with God and one another. Divorce tears apart what God has joined together. While divorce is unavoidable in some cases, it leaves behind the wreckage of broken hearts and hurting children. There are more than 750,000 divorces in the U.S. each year.[2]

  Didn't the Lord make you one with your wife? In body and spirit you are his. And what does he want? Godly children from your union (Malachi 2:15 NLT).

- Pornography is attacking marriage and family, destroying the intimacy God ordained and bringing distrust into a relationship founded on trust. One news source reported that a popular porn site received 30 billion hits in one year.[3] Bitdefender, a security technology company, has reported children under the age of 10 now account for 10 percent of all visitors to porn video sites.[4]

- Sex before marriage robs one of the purity God intended for the marriage union. It can result in out-of-wedlock births and fatherlessness—all of which hurt the chance of having healthy, functional families.

- Adultery destroys marriage's most precious gift—trust! Infidelity is the sexual or intimate engagement with a person outside the marriage of a husband and wife.[5]

- Homosexuality and transgender persuasion are a perversion of God's design and purpose for marriage and family. Transgenderism decimates God's foundational creation of male and female, the two entities needed to have a marriage and produce children. This deception, confusion, and gender identity crisis seeks to damage God's magnificent plan to be fruitful, multiply, and fill the earth. Certainly, those caught in this pain and deception need our love, prayers, and support.[6]

- Abortion attacks marriage and family, ending the purpose of marriage and the life of its offspring. According to the National Right to Life, more than 63 million babies have been aborted in America since 1973.[7] On June 24, 2022, the U.S. Supreme Court overturned Roe v. Wade, the legal verdict that enshrined abortion into law at a federal level, returning the decision of when life will be protected back to the states. Currently, some states in the U.S. have the most extreme abortion laws in the world. These are on par with

China and North Korea and several other countries that allow abortion on demand up until the time of birth.[8]

- Pedophilia, a perverted sexual attraction directed toward children, is attacking marriage and family, as it shatters the futures of young children, even before they enter into marriage. Most experts agree that 500,000 children will be impacted by child sexual abuse every year.[9]

- Domestic abuse attacks marriage and family, as it violates God's command for the husband and wife to love, honor, cherish, and protect each other and their children.

- Here in America, the premeditated destruction of the family has been underway for decades. In 1963, Congressman Albert S. Herlong, Jr. read the 45 Communist Goals for America into the Congressional Record. These goals include the following directives as quoted from the record:[10]

  - Break down cultural standards of morality by promoting pornography and obscenity in books, magazines, motion pictures, radio, and TV.

  - Present homosexuality, degeneracy, and promiscuity as "normal, natural, and healthy."

  - Discredit the family as an institution. Encourage promiscuity and easy divorce.

- Emphasize the need to raise children away from the "negative" influence of parents.

Moving these ungodly ideologies to become accepted as social "norms" is an overarching strategy of satan. And he's using every sphere of culture to work together synergistically to move his agenda forward. If you think about it, currently every one of the seven spheres of culture seems bent on destroying the family—whether it be the entertainment industry, news media, government, education, business, or, sadly, even some churches and denominations.

GOING BACK TO THE GARDEN

God's ultimate end is that the knowledge of His glory would fill the earth as the waters cover the seas (see Hab. 2:14). God has a comprehensive plan for this through the family. "As husband and wife pursue God's way in marriage, they and their children are blessed. They carefully prepare them to exercise godly dominion in every area of society. In due time as these children assume positions of influence in the various spheres of society, these areas are reformed and increasingly reflect God's knowledge and righteousness."[11]

Today, we and our families are reliving the Garden story. Satan breached Adam and Eve's garden paradise through deception, through lying—just as he is working to breach our homes in the same way through deceit and trickery. He wants to destroy our families—and specifically our children—and to prevent or distract us from understanding that we have authority over him and his schemes.

We must not surrender to the slumbering spell of the spirit of this age. Destruction of this diabolical agenda is possible, and it begins at home! Adam and Eve failed at protecting their home. We need to employ all the weapons of warfare God has given us to protect our families. We cannot afford to fail as they did! God gave us stewardship over our homes, to watch over them, and keep the snake (satan) out of the garden!

We do that through prayer and obedience to God's Word. We do that by inviting the presence of the Lord into our homes at the family altar. We do that by teaching our children to faithfully walk and talk with the Lord. We also lovingly model and bring consistent light to God's original design for marriage and family.

We need to recognize the enemy's schemes and do spiritual warfare against the evil infiltrating our households. We also guard over what comes into our homes through TV and the internet, being watchful of our children's choices of friends, the toys and games our children play with, the celebrities they admire, the social media accounts they follow, and the curriculum they study at their schools. (For more guidance, see "Cleansing Your Home from Evil Influences" and "Praying for Your Children's Schools" in the 10-Day Family Prayer Guide in the Appendix.)

We need to pray for God's hedge of protection to surround our children, even and especially when they are not in our presence. (See "Scriptural Prayers for Emerging Generations" in the Appendix for sample prayers to declare over the children in your life.)

Our mandate is the same as Adam and Eve's: to prevent satan from stealing, killing, and destroying our families. We are to "rule, govern, and manage" (ka'bash) and with absolute authority (ma'shal).

Satan is a liar, and he uses lies to destroy lives and cultures. John 8:44 tells us that satan *was a murderer from the beginning, not holding to the truth, for there is no truth in him. When he lies, he speaks his native language, for he is a liar and the father of lies"* (NIV). Satan deceives nations by working through the foundational worldview assumptions that shape a culture.[12]

For these spiritual battles, we need more than scattered shotgun prayers; we need targeted, strategic weapons of prayer to win this war against our family. The word *strategy* is defined as "developing and implementing military operations against an enemy." We need a God-given strategy to take back the family in our nation. Each of us needs a designed strategy for how to defeat the enemy in our own family, and we also need to join forces with other families to claim victory. God has delegated to us the authority to kick satan out of our homes. *"Look, I have given you authority over all the power of the enemy, and you can walk among snakes and scorpions and crush them. Nothing will injure you"* (Luke 10:19 NLT). But the battles for our families must be fought with the *ekklesia*, the family of God.

It's time for the Church to wake up to the all-out assault that has been launched by satan—a battle that is increasingly exposing the evil one's plan to dismantle the family and destroy our children. It's time to get on our knees, then pick up our spiritual weapons and fight with the authority Jesus has given us, in His name.

> *For though we walk in the flesh, we are not waging war according to the flesh. For the weapons of our warfare are not of the flesh but have divine power to destroy strongholds. We destroy arguments and every lofty opinion raised against the knowledge of God, and take every thought captive to obey Christ* (2 Corinthians 10:3-5 ESV).

Always remember, satan is "a usurper, a rebel, a thief that has no right to steal, kill and destroy, but who *will* if not stopped. If we have been delivered from satan's authority and given a higher authority in Christ's name, then we must exercise our authority over the devil's works and power. When we do, God's awesome power will back up our authority."[13]

ACTIVATION: RECOGNIZING THE ENEMY'S SCHEMES

1. Identify ways you see the enemy working to destroy your own family. Do you see evidence that he is attacking your marriage and children? How so? Talk this over with your family. How do you see him trying to dismantle the family sphere in your community, city, or state (including schools, media and entertainment, government, etc.)?

2. Identify Scriptures that apply to these areas of infiltration. Use them as a launching pad to pray about these issues with your spouse and your children, keeping it age appropriate.

3. Together, pray for God's protection for your marriage, household, and family members. (See "Psalm 91 Prayer of Protection for My Family" in the Appendix for more guidance.)

LET'S PRAY

Dear Heavenly Father, please help my family to grow in our understanding of Your principles and purpose for a godly family. Forgive us for adopting the false and harmful models around us. Forgive us for listening to satan's lies. Enable us by Your Holy Spirit to set an example of a family that conforms to Your original design. Empower my family to be part of Your plan to build a nation of strong families that bring honor to Your name. I decree that my family is off-limits to satan—that we are protected by the power and presence of Almighty God. Amen.

CHAPTER 4

THE FAMILY CAN SAVE THE NATION: ONE HOUSEHOLD AT A TIME

But I have raised you up for this very purpose, that I might show you my power and that my name might be proclaimed in all the earth (Exodus 9:16 NIV).

Our nation and the nations around the world are in crisis. We are seeing massive protests, riots, and revolutions. Widespread drought, floods, and fires. Hyperinflation is skyrocketing as undisciplined governments drive up their national debt. Violent crime is increasing in major cities across America. Perhaps even more troubling, we are seeing the rapid loss of personal freedoms and retaliation against those who would confront evil in our day.

In the Bible, when the nation was on the brink of destruction and even annihilation, God had a simple, humble solution. In the darkest, most desperate times He used righteous families to bring deliverance and salvation to the nation.

During the most depraved time in human history—during the days of Noah—God used one family to resist the evil of their day and build the ark. Think also of the stories of Miriam, Aaron, and Moses; Esther and Mordecai; and Joseph, Mary, and Jesus. In these times of national crisis, God used families to bring deliverance.

And He uses not only biological families, but spiritual ones as well. In the Bible, four young men in captivity in Babylon had lost their relatives and any hope of a future family. They were uprooted from their homeland and cruelly turned into eunuchs, depriving them of the chance to ever marry or have children. They lost their natural families but found each other and formed a covenant bond in that foreign land that impacted the greatest empire of their day—through the power of prayer in agreement and bold, courageous action. Joined together as an *ekklesia* in hostile surroundings, the godly lives and faith-filled prayers of Daniel, Shadrach, Meshach, and Abednego changed history.

No matter how bad things are, nuclear families—and covenantal intercessors in the family of God—can make all the difference and turn the tide for a nation!

HOW GOD USES FAMILIES IN TIMES OF CRISIS

Noah and his family heard God's voice and were instructed to prepare an escape before a catastrophic event. Esther, too, heard God—who spoke to her through her cousin and guardian, Mordecai. Risking her own life, she prepared her people in the face of what looked like certain destruction. She called them to prayer, fasting, and seeking the Lord for His deliverance. And He answered and saved them.

We've also seen families in more modern times— seeking God as a family in their place of prayer and worship—take a dramatic role in their uncertain times. In the 1800s, slave families in the American South would gather at night to pray together, often using the black kettles they kept for cooking and washing clothes to muffle the sound of their voices. Turning the pot upside-down on the barn floor, they propped it up with rocks, suspending the pot a few inches above the ground. Then, while lying prostrate or kneeling on the ground, they prayed in a whisper underneath it. Their cruel masters had forbidden them to gather and pray, fearing prayer would give them hope and inspire them to run away. But these enslaved people persevered and would not let threats of punishment and even death deter them from their family altars. They did not presume to pray for their own freedom; they had no hope that it would ever happen. Instead, they risked their own lives to pray for the freedom of the next generation—their children and grandchildren.[1]

During the same time period, Quaker families in the United States played a huge role in forming the Underground Railroad to help slaves escape to freedom. Some made this effort their life's work, creating a system of secret pathways and sanctuary homes, or "stations," along which escaping black slaves from the South could make their way to the free states in the North and Canada.[2] Many Christian historians believe the prayers of a godly remnant of African Americans and white Christian abolitionists birthed revival in America and brought about the demise of slavery.

During World War II in Europe, praying Christian families supported the resistance movement against the Nazis. One of these families was the ten Boom family in the Netherlands, who owned a watchmaking and repair shop in Haarlem. Their daughter, Corrie, became the nation's first licensed woman watchmaker at age 32.

Bible reading, prayer, and family worship were a regular part of the family's life together. Their faith prompted them to engage with their neighbors more deeply than simply fixing watches. At 83, Casper ten Boom and his two daughters—Corrie, then 50, and Betsie, 57—transformed their home into a hiding place. They helped establish an 80-person resistance movement that resulted in the saving of more than 800 Jews from concentration camps and certain death during the Nazi occupation.

Corrie and her sister, Betsie, and their family were members of the Dutch Reformed Church, which protested the Nazi persecution of Jews as an injustice to fellow human beings and a ruthless offense to God. Motivated by intense prayer and a strong faith in God, the ten Boom family not only sheltered Jewish people but encouraged other Christians to open their homes and hide these families. Corrie, Betsie, and their father were eventually caught and imprisoned in the concentration camps where Corrie's sister and father lost their lives.

Besides their immediate impact on the people they saved, the ten Boom family's faith and legacy have inspired millions worldwide through Corrie's now-famous book, *The Hiding Place,* and a movie by the same name. For many years after World War II, Corrie traveled extensively, sharing her story of God's great love and the Jewish people's return to their land of Israel.[3]

What gave these biblical heroes and modern-day families the courage and strength they needed to confront evil in their day? How or where did they get their strategies? What can we learn from them as we face the crises of our own uncertain times?

THE POWER OF THE FAMILY ALTAR

None of the families mentioned above likely had any idea that God would use them to save their nation, much less the world. They simply sought God together, heard from Him, and faithfully and courageously served Him in their sphere of influence. The Bible says of David that he died *"after he had served the purposes of God in his own generation"* (Acts 13:36 ESV). Oh, that families today would fulfill their God-given destinies in this generation! This is what our world needs today! As I write this book, my nation, America, as well as other nations are experiencing a "great shaking." Violent crime is increasing dramatically across the nation. Protests are underway in multiple nations around the world against government overreach. Economists warn of widespread gas, food, and supply chain shortages. A threat of World War III from China and Russia looms on the horizon. Amid all this, the world is recovering from a devastating pandemic that killed millions.

No matter what year you may be reading this book, or what nation you live in, you are likely facing similar crises.

Jesus told His disciples that they needed to stay alert to the times they were living in. He said, *"When evening comes, you say, 'It will be fair weather, for the sky is red,' and in the morning, 'Today it will be stormy, for the sky is red and overcast.' You know how to interpret the appearance of the sky, but you cannot interpret the signs of the times"* (Matt. 16:2-3 NIV).

Jesus conveyed an urgency in the hearts of His disciples, then and now, to be alert, to be like the "men of Issachar," in the Old Testament, "who understood the times" (see 1 Chron. 12:32). Issachar was the name of a tribe of families who lived in the nation of Israel.

These families were gifted by God to recognize what God was doing and knew how to respond. They knew *when* to fight and *how* to fight. They had God's plan.

There is a common theme in all these stories you've just read: together as families, they heard God's voice, discerned His plan, and stepped out in faith and courage to follow the assignment He had given them.

As we spend intentional time with the Lord as families—praying, worshiping, reading, and meditating on His Word—we can hear God's voice and discern His plan. At the family altar, our families can find our God-given assignments and become empowered by His Spirit to confidently step out and do what He is calling us to do. Even if it is difficult and dangerous, He will help us.

Remember that the ten Boom family had the regular habit of family devotions, including concerted praying and worshiping together. They were intimately connected to the Lord in these extraordinary times at the family altar. We surmise they received revelation, direction, courage, and sustaining strength to accomplish their assignment. They learned earlier in their family prayer times how to accept smaller tasks that they embraced with obedience. Because of their earlier faithful adherence to the Lord, they were prepared to act swiftly and decisively in a crisis. They positioned themselves in the Lord and were used mightily for His Kingdom.

IS YOUR FAMILY PREPARED TO BE USED BY GOD?

What might this look like for 21st-century Christian families? Is setting aside time as a family to seek the face of God together even a reality in our fast-paced, chaotic world? After all, we are told and

can readily observe that we live in the most distracted and discon-
nected generation that has ever lived on the planet!

Can we "be still" long enough to wait in His presence, to be
refilled and refreshed, to hear His wisdom for the decisions and
crises we face? Are we in a position to be used by Him when He
calls us (see Ps. 46:10)?

Wherever a family "altar" is burning—where family members
set their hearts to pray, worship, and seek God together—a home
radiates with light that quenches the darkest of cultural depravity or scarcity. *"The light shines in the darkness, and the darkness
can never extinguish it"* (John 1:5 NLT). In times of crisis, God's
fire from our prayer altars will overflow from our homes into the
surrounding community.

When my good friend Arlyn and her family moved into a new
house in a rural area, they had no idea of the spiritual darkness they
were about to encounter. They had looked forward to meeting what
they thought would be friendly new neighbors. However, they discovered that their neighborhood was riddled with alcohol and drug
abuse, domestic violence, and crime. They sometimes saw drug
addicts walking down the road, carrying car parts they were trading
for drugs. Doug and Arlyn began to think they had made a mistake
moving into the neighborhood and wondered if they should leave.

They decided instead to make it a matter of prayer. Rather
than moving away, the Lord led Doug and Arlyn, along with their
five young children, to begin praying together for their neighbors
and their neighborhood. To ensure they didn't leave anyone out,
they drew a map of the streets directly around their home, label-
ing the houses with what little information they knew about their

neighbors—names, observations, impressions, etc. As a family they began to prayer walk their neighborhood regularly. As they passed a house, they would look for clues that might indicate the needs of the families living in them and how they should pray.

At one house, they frequently felt drawn by the Holy Spirit to pause, noting its run-down appearance and sensing a deep need. They prayed.

One day, the police were called there, lights flashing and bullhorn blaring. Doug and Arlyn learned the man of the house—the live-in boyfriend—had been arrested on a domestic violence charge. Doug, Arlyn, and their children prayed fervently for this household that God would do a miracle and bring salvation and healing.

Not long afterward, this same family showed up unexpectedly at Doug and Arlyn's own church. The woman explained, "Our life is a mess and we need help. When I was a small child, a bus would come to our trailer park to pick me up for Sunday school. This was the church it brought me to. I didn't know where else to go."

Doug and Arlyn were able to befriend the couple and lead them to the Lord. After coming to Christ, the couple was married, and the man was set free from a long-time drug and alcohol addiction.

Another set of neighbors, observing the first couple's transformation, also gave their lives to Christ. That husband, too, was delivered from drug addiction. These new, young believers joined Doug and Arlyn's church fellowship and the small-group Bible study that met weekly at Doug and Arlyn's house. The two couples also joined in on the prayer walks.

As they all continued to walk and pray over their neighborhood, the drug house shut down (which also housed an auto theft ring), was demolished, and a beautiful new home was built in its place.

The abandoned house next door to it sold to a Christian missionary family, who moved in and contributed to the changing climate of the neighborhood.

The small group that met at Doug and Arlyn's house continued to grow. Within the group were two sheriff's deputies, one the head of the SWAT team and one the head of the narcotics squad. At the same time, the new believers were still struggling to overcome their addictions and past lifestyles. All were coming together to pray and worship the Lord together—it was a diverse group, to say the least! "We all experienced a mini-revival that changed the course and direction of multiple families, and for our neighborhood," Arlyn said.[4] All because one family built a family "altar" and prayed. (See "Praying for Your Neighborhood" in the Appendix for more guidance on how you can prayer walk your own neighborhood.)

So, back to my earlier question: Are our families prepared to be used by God when He calls us? I suggest:

- We are not prepared if we have not been in the presence of the Lord.

- We are not prepared if we have not attuned our ear to hear His voice.

- We are not prepared if we are accustomed to figuring things out in our natural minds.

- We are not prepared if we are solely operating in our own strength.

- We are not prepared if we make decisions without consulting God.

- We are not prepared if we are isolated, self-sufficient, and self-willed.

Realistically, I think we can agree that many, if not most of us,
are woefully unprepared to deal with difficult or uncertain times,
for both the challenges and opportunities that come our way to
make a difference in our families and in our world. Most of us have
thought about how to prepare for storms. We have seen and felt the
suffering of women, men, and children, and the aged and the weak,
caught in hurricanes, tsunamis, and droughts. But most of us, par-
ticularly in the Western world, have never thought about preparing ourselves—practically or spiritually—for the possibility that
hard times will come against us, storms or otherwise. Who knows
whether we, too, might someday face hardships that many people
in other parts of the world have endured at various times, such as
economic hardship, political or religious persecution, or even war.

For the ten Boom family, living in 1942 Holland, the Nazi
deportation of Jews presented them a weighty challenge as they
tried to meet the needs of their friends and neighbors. This was
not a stretch for them, however. Their lives had been characterized
by ministering to those in need for years. In the lean years following
World War I, the ten Booms had started filling the empty rooms in
their home with refugee children, orphans, and missionary children
as a part of their lifestyle of the family altar, which included prayer,
worship, and serving their community.[5]

While the ten Boom family's courageous decision to begin
hiding Jews in their home was a significant one, it was simply the
next logical step in a pattern of life characterized by prioritizing
the family altar of worship and prayer and serving those in need
around them.

ACTIVATION: PUTTING FEET TO YOUR PRAYERS

1. Talk with your family about the causes that stir passion in each of your hearts. Ask each family member to share what they are most concerned about. It may be a heart for children without a family, hurting neighbors, or friends at school. If you have young children who share something that seems trivial, try not to make light of it. The fact that they are engaging with the family in this time is hugely important. Write down everyone's concerns. (See "Your Family's Future and Calling" within the 10-Day Family Prayer Guide in the Appendix for more guidance.)

2. Pray and ask the Lord if there is something He is asking your family to do about the problem. Commit to doing whatever the Lord asks of you.

3. Write down what you hear the Lord saying to you and revisit this the next time your family gathers for a meal or for prayer.

LET'S PRAY

Lord, even as we saw in the early days of this nation and around the world, we pray that families—including ours—would return to daily prayer, worship, Bible reading, and sharing stories of Your faithfulness. We ask You to help us prioritize seeking You together as a family, allowing Your Spirit to draw us closer to You and each other. Fill us with Your Spirit and give us the strength and courage we need to be Your agents of peace and action in times of crisis and uncertainty in our nation and world. We declare, in Jesus' name, that our family will be a city on a hill, a sanctuary of God's light and love wherever You plant us or send us. We decree that Your light in us will shine brightly, so the world may see and give You glory (Matt. 5:14-16). Amen.

PART TWO

ENCOUNTERING THE LORD ALONE AND WITH OTHERS

CHAPTER 5

HOW TO SPEND TIME ALONE WITH GOD: CREATING A PLACE TO ENCOUNTER HIM

Above everything else guard your heart, because from it flow the springs of life (Proverbs 4:23 ISV).

When we talk about an "altar," the first place to start is with the one we build connecting us with the Lord. In reality, the family altar starts here—with us—our own intimate relationship with our Heavenly Father. This relational connection begins with our own life before it translates into anything memorable or lasting for the rest of our family.

In Washington, DC, our friends Jon and Jolene Hamill lead a thriving ministry focused on spiritual turnaround for the nation. Jon shares a story that illustrates how breakthrough in our family starts first in our own heart, our own personal prayer altar:

It was early Christmas morning in 2015 when my son Jonathan knocked at our bedroom door. My first thought was a flashback to his childhood, when an eager knock meant our kids could no longer wait to open their gifts. But Jonathan was an adult now. And it soon became apparent he had much more important things on his mind.

The conversation went something like this: "Dad, I wanted you to be the first to know. I came home last night! Well, this morning, actually."

"Came home?"

"Yeah. To Jesus! Dad, I had an encounter..."

It turned out that early Christmas morning, the Lord Jesus Christ literally appeared to our son in a vision. With hands outstretched and open arms, the Son of God compelled our son to "return home!" Of course Jonathan said yes. He recommitted his life to Christ that very moment, and remains strong for the Lord today.

It was exactly one year earlier, on Christmas Day of 2014, that my wife Jolene and I felt God prompting us to commit to a year of prayer for our son and daughter. We had honestly been focusing our ministry efforts on securing a national turnaround. But on Christmas Day in 2014, the Lord spoke to my heart that before we could legitimately partner with Him for a turnaround for the nation, we first needed to focus on a turnaround for our own family.

That's how "Turnaround Tuesday" was born—our weekly day of prayer for our kids who were not walking with the Lord.

For background, Jonathan had fallen away from the Lord while attending a non-denominational "Christian" college in the Northeast. Professors had introduced him to schools of philosophy that completely negated his faith, which was crazy, because from his youth, Jonathan had maintained an incredibly close relationship with the Lord. He went to this college literally on fire.

Students at the college introduced him to unholy fire—drugs especially. By graduation he had utterly disengaged from faith in Jesus, continuing down a dark path spiritually for several years following.

When the Lord first spoke to me about Turnaround Tuesday, He gave me a Scripture I was already so familiar with I could recite it in my sleep. But due to my own pain over the situations with our children, the love that resonates through this message was very distant from my own heart. God was challenging me to engage in a way I did not want to, or even feel I could—to become vulnerable to my children again. "He will turn the hearts of the fathers back to their children and the hearts of the children to their fathers, so that I will not come and strike the land with complete destruction" (Mal. 4:6 NASB).

Pray for our children? I thought it was all about a turnaround for them. But in reading this verse, I suddenly realized the first "family altar" God wanted to restore was the altar of my own heart! He wanted to turn my heart back to my sons and daughters—to genuinely forgive and open my heart to truly love again. Prayer comes easily when this happens.

The good news is that He is available to help us through this process. He floods us with a love that transcends even family disappointments and pain. He helps us pray...and we begin to see His turnaround!

This story encompasses all the necessary stones in the family altar: it started with Jon's personal altar, moved to the marriage altar, and then to the family altar as other family members joined Turnaround Tuesday. Finally, it reached into the extended family as it moved globally and began to touch and transform families everywhere.

ALTARS MARK ENCOUNTERS

As you build and sustain your own personal altar where you encounter God, you will begin to live in a continual sense of God's tangible presence. This is the special meeting place where you will worship, pray, and hear from God's living Word. You will enjoy the pleasure of knowing God intimately. In this relational exchange, as Jon Hamill experienced, your heart will become tender and more vulnerable, yielded, and surrendered to His Holy Spirit. You will discover how to better follow Him, trust Him, and allow His life to flow through you. This shared communion through Christ Jesus is the cornerstone of the family altar.

An extraordinary and powerful transaction happens when you set aside a regular time to meet with God personally—one to One.

In these unhurried settings, you can focus your heart to engage in worshiping the Lord, centering upon His goodness, mercy, and faithfulness. As you pull aside from the demands of life and focus on Jesus, you can hear from the Holy Spirit more clearly and receive direction and peace.

Jesus taught His disciples the importance of "abiding in the Vine" in John 15. He revealed what it would be like to experience communion and closeness with Him, a deep place of finding rest, peace, security, safety, life, and strength. In this abiding, all other loves besides Him fade away. All "idols"—things in our life apart from Him in which we find identity, security, or comfort—are cast aside. This is a passionate returning to "home," abiding in the Vine, the place of first love (see Eph. 3:15-20).

It is in this place that His unquenchable fire will ignite the flame of revival in your own heart and then spread to those around you.

HOW TO BUILD YOUR PERSONAL ALTAR

In modern times, we do not have physical altars made of stone, like Abraham and others built in the Old Testament. Instead, in the New Testament, the apostle Peter says that we, individually, are *"like living stones…to offer spiritual sacrifices acceptable to God through Jesus Christ"* (1 Pet. 2:5 ESV).

A personal altar is not necessarily a physical location. *We* are the altar. *We* are the living stones. Our heart is the altar that we want to keep burning for God. It's the place we focus, yield, and surrender to Him. There is an eternal flame that burns upon our heart, awakening us to His presence and purpose.

Where would you like to go to meet with God (either personally or as a family)? You may have a place you enjoy—one filled with an atmosphere of peace and security, an inviting place where you can meet with God, worship Him, and enjoy His presence. Perhaps it's a chair near a window where you can watch the sunrise, a bench in a flower garden where you can focus on the beauty of nature, or simply your kitchen table with a cup of coffee in hand. Yet, always keep in mind that the primary place of the altar is your heart. The physical location is secondary. The goal is to discover that quiet place where you can come into communion with Him, hear His gentle whisper, and go away changed (see 1 Kings 19:12).

INTIMACY WITH THE FATHER AND HEARING HIS VOICE

Hearing God's voice is essential to nurturing your relationship with Him. Today we all need to be able to discern the Father's direction more than ever. One of the functions of the Holy Spirit is that He will show us the things to come (see John 16:13). This is not only life-giving; it can be lifesaving!

One early morning a pastor living with his family in the foothills of Colorado was awakened and heard the Lord say, "Take your family and get out of town *now!*" He knew it was the Spirit of God speaking to him, so he did as he was told. Within a couple hours of gathering up his family and driving away from their home, a flash flood came down the canyon wiping out the entire area. The flood not only swept away his home but the very land it sat on. The pastor and his family were saved because he heard God's voice and obeyed.

You might be asking how this pastor knew that God was speaking to him. Jesus tells us in John 10:4 that *"his sheep follow him because they know his voice"* (NIV). We can easily recognize the voices of our friends and family because we know them—this is also true of God! His voice is just as unique and recognizable as any other person's. The question is, how well do you know Him and listen to His voice? The more you spend time with Him, the more easily you will recognize Him when He speaks to you!

I find most often that God speaks to me by His Spirit through His Word, the Bible (see 2 Tim. 3:16-17). Because God is the same yesterday, today and forever, His Word applies to any situation today just as much as it did centuries ago (see Heb. 13:8). Even if God doesn't speak to you directly out of Scripture, if you know the Bible, you can recognize what *is* and *is not* God's will for you (see Prov. 3:5-6). God's voice will never contradict His Word (see Ps. 119:105; John 1:1).

I've also learned to be open to the different ways God speaks. Sometimes God speaks through other people, as in wise counsel. He may give you a dream, a mental picture, a timely song, or the feeling of peace (or restlessness) when you pray about a situation. God's Word tells us the peace of God will act as an umpire in our hearts—giving us a "green light" or "red light" (see Col. 3:15).

MOVING FROM FEAR TO FAITH

The current chaos in our world and the challenges in our personal lives and families can evoke fear and anxiety. Yet the Lord has made a way for us to live free of fear (see John 14:27). We find God's peace in His presence, and His Word is an anchor in the midst of life's storms. I have found that if my time with the Lord wanes, I can lapse into fear and worry.

At the altar—our time spent with God—we have the opportunity to surrender those troubling things to Him and receive His peace in return, the *"peace of God that surpasses all understanding,"* which *will guard your hearts and minds in Christ Jesus*" (Phil. 4:6-7 NET). As we meditate on God's promises, His Word gives us confidence and assurance (see Isa. 54:13-14). Faith comes by hearing and hearing by the Word of God (see Rom. 10:17). (See "Praying God's Prayer Promises" in the Appendix for more guidance.)

When I read and pray God's Word, I am quickened with faith. His Word is alive and sharper than a two-edged sword (see Heb. 4:12). Sometimes I write the Scriptures down on index cards or Post-it® notes and place them where I can see them and be reminded of their truth—maybe on the dash of my car or on my refrigerator—verses like:

> *Have I not commanded you? Be strong and courageous. Do not be afraid; do not be discouraged, for the Lord your God will be with you wherever you go* (Joshua 1:9 NIV).

> *"For I know the plans I have for you," declares the Lord, "plans to prosper you and not to harm you, plans to give you hope and a future"* (Jeremiah 29:11 NIV).

Praying and meditating on Scripture helps us take our eyes off the bigness of our problems and focus on the greatness of God. When Jesus was teaching His disciples to pray, do you remember how He began? *"Our Father."* He started with *God*—not the problem. We get the proper perspective when we look at our problems through the lens of God's power and might. (For more guidance see "Praying Scripture" within the 10-Day Family Prayer Guide in the Appendix.)

YOUR CHILDREN ARE WATCHING YOU

Establishing your own personal prayer time with God is laying the first stone in your marriage and family altar. Whether you realize it or not, you are being watched! Your example is a testimony to your spouse and children. You are demonstrating what a close relationship with the Lord looks like.

I inadvertently discovered this when our daughter, Nicole, was a preschooler. At that time, my life was hectic raising her and working full-time in ministry. With our growing work headquartered in our home, I often felt my personal and family life was infringed upon. Our photocopier was stationed in our master bedroom and the kitchen table served as my desk. My time was consumed serving as a personal assistant to my husband, developing my teaching ministry, trying to keep our home clean and organized, and running after a three-year-old.

It seemed the only time I had to spend alone with the Lord was very early in the morning. I would often awake at 4:00 a.m. to slip out of bed and tip-toe down the hall past Nicole's room to the living room couch to pray while peering out the picture window into the quiet night sky. No matter how carefully I crept past Nicole's door, it was usually only a matter of minutes until I heard the pitter-patter of little feet and saw her silhouette appear in the doorway with a pillow and blanket dragging behind.

"What are you doing, Mommy?" she would ask.

"I'm praying, honey! This is Mommy's time to talk to God."

At first I tried to coerce her into going back to bed. At this stage in my life I didn't recognize I was about to miss an excellent opportunity to invite Nicole into my "prayer closet"—to demonstrate my love for God and model a life of prayer. After realizing that all of my prayer time would be used up in a battle of getting her back to bed, I began inviting Nicole to sit quietly with me during my prayer time. Wrapped in a warm blanket, she would snuggle next to me and listen as I whispered my prayers to God. Sometimes she would fall asleep beside me. More often than not, the first glimmer of morning sun would find us sitting together in the presence of the Lord.

Hal, on the other hand, would usually go for long prayer walks in the evenings. Nicole still talks about how she enjoyed riding on her daddy's shoulders as he walked our neighborhood and poured out his heart to God.[1]

Many times, I've heard it said that prayer is more "caught" than "taught." If this is true, then welcoming children into our personal prayer time, or at least letting them observe it from time to time, is one of the best ways to ensure that we pass on a legacy of prayer to the next generation.

In his book *Teaching Children to Pray,* Keith Wooden says, "A 'prayer closet' that is open to the intrusive chatter of children may be the best opportunity you have to demonstrate your reverence and love for God. Invite them into your Holy of Holies to savor the presence of the Lord with you."[2] We must let our children see and hear us pray. Children need to know that God lives in their home and that He is available to them.

We may pray all the time, but if our children never see us pray it can hinder their learning process. Children are always watching us, and our actions often have a much more profound effect on their lives, even more than the words we speak.

TIPS FOR YOUR PRAYER TIME

Every relationship needs time together to grow and deepen. A Christian's relationship with God is no different. It takes time with God to get to know Him better, to hear His heart, and to foster intimacy with Him.

Jesus set the example for us. He regularly got away alone to spend time with His Heavenly Father. Most of us want to foster this relationship, but sometimes we aren't sure how to make it happen. Today's busy lifestyle makes regular time with God challenging, but it can be done with planning and commitment.

So, once you've decided to spend time with God regularly, what's next? What will it look like? How can we get the most out of the time we do have to spend with God? Here are some tips to help you establish an intentional, meaningful time with the Lord:

- Establish a regular place and time: If you know when and where you will meet with God daily, you are much more likely to do it. Build it into your daily schedule. If this is new for you, start small, commit to it, and God will grow it.

- Organize your "tool" box: Gather your tools (Bible, reading plan, journal, pen, etc.) and keep them together in your designated spot so you'll always be prepared. I've found having a reading plan dramatically increases the chance of me staying in the Word regularly. Without a plan, reading stays haphazard at best.

- Minimize distractions: Though it's not possible to eliminate them all, you can take steps to help maintain your focus. Email and social media are my biggest distractions. I had to determine not to open my laptop until after my quiet time. What competes for your attention the most?

- Start with prayer: Ask God to speak to you and bring a fresh revelation of His Word to you. Thank Him for being tangibly present with you.

- Begin to read the Bible: Remember, your purpose is to communicate with God. The Bible is the primary way God speaks to us. Take your time; don't read hastily just to get through the passage. Stop and let God speak to you.

- Meditate on the passage: Meditation is not emptying your mind; it is deep thinking on spiritual truths. As you read, linger over verses that impact you. Ask God questions and "listen" for His answers.

- Pray as you read: Time with God should be interactive. Respond to God as He speaks to you through His Word. Reading and praying creates a conversation with God. I often stop and pray back to God the Scripture I've just read. Praying through the book of Proverbs is something I do regularly.

- Journal: Read with a pen in hand. Record what God says to you and how you will respond. Writing can help you stay focused on God and His voice. You can also read your thoughts later to be reminded of something God taught you, an answered prayer, a time you felt His presence, etc.

- Memorize: Commit to memorizing verses to which God calls your special attention. Knowing Scripture by heart helps us guard against sin, reminds us of God's promises, provides guidance, and allows us to meditate on God's Word anywhere and anytime.

- Live it out: Follow through with whatever God says to you through His Word and prayer. It may be repentance. It may be a change in behavior. It may be a specific action you need to take.

ACTIVATION: ESTABLISHING YOUR PERSONAL PRAYER ALTAR

1. Find a comfortable place where you can be undistracted and completely quiet for at least 15 minutes. You might choose a place outside or where you can look out a window.

2. Begin by tuning out the rest of the world and inviting God to join you. Of course, He is always present everywhere at all times, but He likes to be welcomed! Invite Him to fill you with His Spirit and speak to you through His Word. If you are able to see outdoors, you can express praise to God for His beautiful gift of creation or pray for your next-door neighbor. At this point, you don't need to worry about fulfilling any expectations; just focus on the goodness and faithfulness of God.

3. Open your Bible and begin to read God's Word. If you don't already have a reading plan, you might

start with reading the Psalms, a few every day, and allowing the words of the psalmists to inspire your thoughts and your conversation with God. They are full of heartfelt expressions on a number of topics. You may well find that the Holy Spirit speaks to you personally through them.

4. Next, bring your needs and concerns to God, thanking Him that He is already at work in those situations. If you're feeling hopeless about a situation, try approaching God with gratitude instead of complaint or despair. I find that if I turn my requests into thanksgiving, it significantly affects how I view those situations. For example, "I thank You, Lord, that I do not need to worry because You have said You will meet all of my needs according to Your riches in glory in Christ Jesus" (see Phil. 4:19).

If you are praying in the morning, close your prayer time by asking the Lord to lead and guide you throughout the day. If it is evening, thank God for what He did that day and give Him the next one. It's interesting that the Hebrew day starts at 6:00 p.m. the night before. It's an excellent way to prepare both practically and spiritually for the day ahead!

LET'S PRAY

Heavenly Father, I desire to have a fresh, life-giving, two-way conversation with You every day. You are my Best Friend and I choose You to be first place in my life. Draw me to the Quiet Place with You today, the still waters that quiet my soul. I determine to set aside every distraction and have a meaningful time with You when I can hear Your voice and discern what You are saying to me. I lay before You every fear, anxious thought, and concern, and ask You to give me Your perspective and heart for every circumstance I face. As I release these things to You, fill me with faith, hope, and expectation now and for the future. This day, I proclaim: Holy Spirit, come! Amen!

CHAPTER 6

ENRICHING YOUR MARRIAGE THROUGH PRAYER: MORE INTIMACY, LESS CONFLICT

Two people are better off than one, for they can help each other succeed. ...Three are even better, for a triple-braided cord is not easily broken (Ecclesiastes 4:9,12 NLT).

A young Christian couple on the brink of divorce scheduled an appointment with the pastor who married them. They asked the pastor what advice he could give them that would save their crumbling marriage. The pastor asked if they had been meeting faithfully every day to read God's Word and pray together. They confessed that they had not.

"Go home and start with that—and give your marriage one more try," he said. Though it felt like an impossible task, they agreed to try it.

One night, as the couple was praying and reading God's Word together, the husband ran across 1 Corinthians 13:

> *Love is patient and kind. Love is not jealous or boastful or proud or rude. It does not demand its own way. It is not irritable, and it keeps no record of being wronged. It does not rejoice about injustice but rejoices whenever the truth wins out. Love never gives up, never loses faith, is always hopeful, and endures through every circumstance* (1 Corinthians 13:4-7 NLT).

He was struck to the core.

As tears filled his eyes, he laid down the Bible, put his arms around his wife, and begged her forgiveness. He apologized for the cruel things he had said and done to her. Without hesitation, she forgave him. With tears running down her face, she asked him to forgive her for the ways she had lived in bitterness and resentment. The young couple prayed and sobbed in each other's arms as they experienced the freedom of forgiveness and Jesus' promise, *"For where two or three gather in my name, there am I with them"* (Matt. 18:20 NIV).[1]

THE COUPLE THAT PRAYS TOGETHER, STAYS TOGETHER

What are the benefits when couples pray together? The family that prays together really is more likely to stay together, as we see so beautifully illustrated in the previous story. In fact, a study by the University of Virginia has found that prayer leads to intimacy, helps couples become closer, and can help end disagreements.[2]

Praying couples enjoy immeasurable results and significant benefits in their marriage, which include:

1. *Permanency and Harmony*

Nearly half of all marriages today fail. The couples who take time to pray together, calling upon their Heavenly Father to unravel the issues of the day, find continual healing, peace, and His presence in their marriage.

2. *Unity*

In marriage, couples must discover how to mesh their dreams, desires, attitudes, assumptions, and needs with those of their spouse. This can sometimes cause strife. When you pray together, calling upon God for His direction and solutions, He unites you in His perfect plan—you are drawn into unity with the Lord and one another.

3. *Emotional Intimacy*

Just as the beauty of physical intimacy reaffirms your oneness, so does praying together. When you pray as a couple, inviting God's Spirit into the conversation, you can experience closer communion with the Lord and each other. You can learn so much about one another by sharing your needs and agreeing with each other in prayer for God's answers. Keep in mind this powerful principle: we become intimate *with* whom we pray, *for* whom we pray, and *to* whom we pray.

4. *Inviting God into Your Marriage*

For a marriage to be lasting and fulfilling, three participants must be involved: the wife, the husband, and the Lord. Ecclesiastes 4 says, "*Two people are better than one...moreover, a three-stranded cord is not quickly broken*" (Eccles. 4:9,12 NET).

All marriages have challenges because they are made up of two imperfect people. But if you add the presence of a perfect God, then you have unlimited possibilities for drawing closer to what God intended for marriage. The more you pray together and invite the Lord into your relationship, the more you will see Him perfecting the flaws and smoothing out the rough places in your lives.

5. *Changed Relationships*

My husband, Hal, and I are living proof that any relationship can benefit from praying together and experience God's healing. A husband and wife certainly can't change each other, but God can change them both if they invite Him to do so. No matter what a couple struggles with, they can see things turn around if they keep reaching out to God together.

HUMILITY HEALS HEARTS AND CLOSES THE DOOR TO THE ENEMY

It takes humility to admit you're wrong and that you have hurt someone you love, but it's the only path to true reconciliation. Years ago, Hal and I learned a powerful model that begins by taking that courageous step. Following an argument or hurtful disagreement, Hal would come to me and express that he was sorry for his unkind words and ask my forgiveness. Then he would lay his hand on my heart and pray something like: "Lord, I've been an instrument of pain and wounding to my wife; now I ask You to make me an instrument of healing to her. Forgive me for hurting her, heal the wounds that I've inflicted, and restore our love and closeness." Then using the same model, I would pray a similar prayer from my heart for Hal.

We learned never to hold on to anger or resentment but to reconcile as soon as possible.

> *"In your anger do not sin": Do not let the sun go down while you are still angry, and do not give the devil a foothold* (Ephesians 4:26-27 NIV).

As these prayers greatly impacted our relationship, we realized we needed to include our daughter in this healing prayer. So, when things got tense in our home, we began to talk to Nicole about it. If we were arguing, we let her know we knew our arguing hurt her and made her afraid. We told her we had asked each other for forgiveness. Then we asked her to forgive us, too.

The time always ended with one of us putting our hand over Nicole's heart and praying that God would heal the wounds we had inflicted and asking Him to restore our family's intimacy again. Besides drawing us closer together as a family, Nicole now had a model for healing and reconciliation through prayer that she could one day use with her own marriage and family—and she does. This kind of humble and sincere reconciliation quickly closes the door to the infiltration of the enemy into our families by preventing bitterness from festering.

My good friend Cindy Jacobs tells about the unique way she and her husband pray together:

> Mike and I have a special place we go to pray together when we're facing desperate situations; when one of our family members is seriously ill or there is no money in the bank and bills are piled high. It's the place we go when we're having a bitter disagreement and both of us feel we are RIGHT!

There's a padded bench at the foot of our bed. It's not fancy and there are no decorations, but this is our special place. We simply kneel down there and take hands. I won't lie and say this is an easy thing to do when you're having a disagreement. But we just do it, even if we don't feel like it. We look each other in the eyes and tell our side of the story. We listen to each other and then we pray.

This can be a VERY effective form of marriage counseling. For one reason, it's difficult to feel proud or angry when you're kneeling, and even more so when you're looking right in the eyes of the person you love. Usually, one or both of us see we were wrong. From this humble vantage point, the things we were quarreling over can look very small and make one feel quite foolish for the way we acted. We ask forgiveness, our love for each other is rekindled, and our peace and unity are restored.[3]

Even if you think your marriage is on the brink of divorce, if you both are willing, you can pray a simple prayer and ask God to heal your marriage and restore your love for one another. He will do it! As you come together, simply ask one another's forgiveness. (This is not a time to rehearse all your offenses toward one another. Simply be willing to forgive.) Then, together, command the "destroyer" to take his hands off your marriage and get out of your home, in Jesus' name! You may not "feel" like doing this. But if you have tried everything else and are desperate to save your marriage, why not try it God's way? (See "Praying Breakthrough for a Troubled Marriage" in the Appendix for more guidance.)

IDEAS FOR THINGS TO PRAY ABOUT WITH YOUR SPOUSE

You might be asking, "What should we pray about when we come together?" Many couples like to have their own private time of prayer separate from the rest of the family. This allows them to talk and pray about discreet or confidential matters relating to their marriage, extended family, or friends.

While you may not cover all of these topics, I've included a few ideas you may like to incorporate into your prayers:

- Your marriage relationship: unity of purpose, strengthening, healing, more quality time together, spiritual nourishment, refreshment, and rejuvenation of the love you have for each other

- Your children: their school, friends, outside influences, attitudes of heart, their calling, for God to bring forth their spiritual giftings and destiny with godly character

- Your finances: where to give and how much, new opportunities for income, wisdom in spending, career path and job advancement, your employer and work environment

- Deliverance from unhealthy lifestyles: for the Lord to set you and your family free of bondages and help you to stay free

- Forgiveness: for broken relationships with God and others, repentance for any breakdown in relating to your extended families (in-laws, parents, relatives, close friends) on both sides of the relationship

- Contend with forces of darkness: spiritual forces attempting to bring confusion in your relationships, business, or ministry

- The Church: an atmosphere of "open heavens," liberty in proclaiming the Gospel, revival, equipping of families, serving the community, reaching those who do not know Christ. (See "Seven Powerful Life-Giving Prayers for Your Church" in the Appendix for more guidance.)

If you are parents, the most significant and influential role you and your spouse have is praying faithfully over the destiny of your children. Because of your close relationship, you know your children better than anyone and can discern when and how they most need prayer. (See "Praying God's Promises for My Children" in the Appendix for more guidance.)

Nate, whom I mentioned earlier, shares how he and his wife stay in tune with each other and the Lord to pray for their five children:

My wife and I know the spiritual pulse of our kids. We know who is responding to what. We are in tune with the spiritual sensitivity of each of our children. She homeschools our kids in the day, and at night, when she is at work, I lead them in family worship and prayer.

On more than one occasion, my wife and I will have the same thought about the same child. We'll sit in bed at night and pray for that child because we can see how that one is treating his brother or sister. When we do this, without fail, we begin to see that child's heart become soft. Several times we've seen immediate changes within a week—a soft heart, a willingness to say they are sorry. We'll see a recognition of their need for the Lord to change their heart. We'll see a new kindness or helpfulness around the house, a desire to obey rather than grudging obedience.

No family is perfect. But you can take the problems in life and, with prayer, turn them into opportunities to handle life's problems in a godly way and teach your children to do the same.

If you're convinced you'd like to make prayer a part of your marriage relationship, don't wait. You can start today. Here are some simple guidelines for a successful time in worship and prayer together.

- Keep it simple. Simple sometimes means short. You don't need to pray for two hours; sometimes ten minutes is a good start! I remember speaking at a conference in Dallas one Saturday on the topic of "Fire on the Family Altar." Afterward, an elderly woman pulled up a chair next to me during the lunch break. "What you said today is so true," she told me. "Over 20 years ago, my husband and I started doing this. We'd hold hands and pray for each other every night in bed before we dropped off to sleep. It saved our marriage!"

- Be vulnerable. Don't hold back from sharing your heart. Be willing to be transparent about what is going on in your life, including your thoughts and emotions. Vulnerability and transparency will build intimacy between you and God and with each other.

- Pray positive, life-giving prayers over your spouse. Finger-pointing leads to destruction, but speaking the life-giving promises of God produces godly results. Allow God who started the good work in you and your spouse to continue to make the changes (see Phil. 1:6). Remember, *"Death and life are in the power of the tongue"* (Prov. 18:21 ESV). Hearing someone pray faith-filled words over your life is hugely encouraging. These are the kinds of prayers that are so healing and transformative to a marriage. (See "A Morning Prayer for My Wife" or "A Morning Prayer for My Husband" in the Appendix for more guidance.)

- Do it consistently. You may agree as a couple to establish a daily or weekly time to pray together. That doesn't have to be the only time you pray together; spontaneity is good too! I love how regular times of prayer can become a lifestyle of praying together at any time at any place.

WHAT IF YOUR SPOUSE IS RESISTANT TO PRAYING WITH YOU?

It is not unusual for one spouse to be more enthusiastic about praying together than the other. For example, your spouse may not know the Lord or believe as you do. If this is your situation, pray and bring your spouse's needs before the Lord. Take hold of God's promises and proclaim that you both will serve God's redemptive purpose. Ask God for all He has for you together. Also proclaim prophetically that your marriage will be a shining testimony of His love and faithfulness to others around you.

Sometimes one spouse might feel the other is a "better pray-er," causing a bit of intimidation. Or they might feel their spouse is so long-winded that they can't get a prayer in edgewise. Try to defuse this argument by keeping your prayers short and not setting the bar too high as to the length and substance of your prayer time. Remember, a short, simple prayer together can be just as profound as a long one, maybe even more so.

A first step might be to ask your spouse to pray a short prayer *for* you, instead of *with* you, whenever there is a need in your life. Maybe when you're sick, or have a concern at work, you can ask, "Honey, would you please pray for me about _____?"

Don't press the issue. Let me encourage you to be gentle with your request and not try to pressure your spouse into praying with you. If they are resistant and unwilling, just start praying for your spouse and marriage on your own. You may want to find a friend who also wants to pray for their spouse. Form a partnership to pray together for each other's marriage.

What if you're the one who is feeling unwilling? As a follower of Christ, and an otherwise praying person, if you are reluctant to pray with your spouse, this might be an excellent opportunity to examine your heart. Ask yourself, *Why am I hesitant to pray with my spouse? Is there some unforgiveness in my heart? Am I withholding or afraid of intimacy with my spouse? If so, why?* Ask the Lord to reveal what the blockage is. Do you need to forgive your spouse and be healed? Ask the Lord to forgive you, and you may want to ask your spouse to forgive you. You might discover, after doing this, that you have a completely new outlook on praying together.

KEEPING "COUPLE PRAYER" GOING

After our daughter Nicole grew up and married, Hal's and my regular "set aside" times to pray together waned for a while. We might pray when we were driving along together, or if we or a family member had some special need, but our prayer times together weren't intentional or consistent.

One day we began to feel the Lord drawing us to reestablish our family altar, even though we no longer had children living at home. We started by setting aside an hour every Sunday evening to pray. However, soon our prayer times expanded to more evenings during the week. Sometimes we'd spend the first part of our time together reading Scripture or an inspiring Christian book. We often went through a chapter a night, taking turns reading. These stories always catalyzed our faith and gave us new insights to pray about.

I'm continually amazed at all the benefits of praying together. One night I asked Hal this question: "What has God been saying to you this week?" It wasn't a leading question. I didn't have anything particular in mind. However, when he told me what he sensed God was saying to him, I was stunned. I had heard the same thing from the Lord just a few days earlier. It had only been an impression. And I most certainly would have let it slip by had I not asked Hal that question and he'd confirmed what I'd heard. Now, asking each other what we hear God saying is something we always do when we meet up for prayer. It helps us stay on the same page with each other and, more importantly, with the Lord.

ACTIVATION: ESTABLISHING YOUR MARRIAGE PRAYER ALTAR

1. Set aside 15 minutes to pray together with your spouse. Consider starting by discussing how God has answered your prayers in the past or how you sense He is leading your life, family, and marriage.

2. Remind each other of promises God has made to you, Scripture passages God's Spirit has spoken into your life, stories that have been inspirational to you, or prophetic words you've received either as individuals or as a couple. Pray these promises and prophetic words out loud together. As you build your marriage altar, these will strengthen your faith to believe for more of God's favor and open doors.

3. Start a couple's prayer journal and keep a list of your prayer requests. Don't forget to record the answers. These are great memories of God's faithfulness you will want to remember and pass on to your family.

LET'S PRAY

Lord God, thank You for being the Author of life and the Designer of marriage. Marriage is a beautiful picture of Your relationship with us, and worthy of honor because You instituted it. We invite you afresh into our marriage; breathe new life into our relationship. Help us to love each other as You love Your Church. Help us demonstrate Jesus' pure, unselfish love for each other. Forgive us for trying to figure things out on our own rather than bringing our challenges to You. From now on, we commit to praying for each other, with each other, and for our family. It is our heart to make praying together the foundation of our lives together with You. I decree that my marriage is a strong, triple-braided cord, three strands that cannot be broken—husband, wife, and the Lord God Almighty! Amen.

CHAPTER 7

GETTING STARTED WITH FAMILY PRAYER: WAYS TO ENGAGE EVERYONE

It is written, "My house shall be a house of prayer" (Luke 19:46 ESV).

O ur first home was a small cottage-style house, red brick with brown wooden trim and a shaker roof. It was only 1,100 square feet in size, but we were excited that it would be our very own. Buying the house was a miracle because we had no money for a down payment and no credit rating to secure a mortgage, but God miraculously provided.

What I remember most about the house is not its homey exterior, but the beauty of what went on inside—sitting on the living room sofa praying over our daughter's future, praying around the kitchen table, asking for "our daily bread" and preparing to pay bills, in the small home office asking God for direction and open doors for the ministry, and sitting around Nicole's bed at night, praying for her peace and protection.

When Jesus said, *"My house shall be called a house of prayer"* (Matt. 21:13 ESV), He was not just talking about the "church." He was talking about our homes—and let's not forget that the first churches were in homes. Jesus wants to be more than someone we worship and talk about on Sunday, but the One we worship and talk to all the time—personally and as families. He wants our homes to be "a house of prayer" where He is invited into every aspect of our family relationships and life together.

GETTING STARTED

You might be thinking, *This sounds pretty powerful. How can my family create times of prayer like this?*

Many families find that the biggest obstacle to praying together is just getting started. Your family might not be accustomed to praying together. Maybe you only pray sporadically and would like to make your time together more meaningful. So it's helpful to have a plan. In my book, *The Prayer Saturated Family*, I talk about how to jump-start family prayer. Some questions that inevitably arise are:

- "Who's going to lead the prayer time?"
- "When and where shall we meet?"
- "We've never done this before; what should it look like?"
- "What are we going to pray about?"
- "What if not everyone in the family wants to come?"

These are all great questions!

Julie was asking these same questions when she started to call her family together for prayer. She initiated a family meeting to ask each family member to give input into what their prayer altar would look like. Since they had children of several ages, Julie and her husband, Greg, wanted everyone to participate; so, they decided that they would all take turns leading different components of the prayer time.

Seated around the table (and enjoying chocolate sundaes) they planned their prayer meetings: they decided on the format of their family prayer altar, what kinds of things they would pray about, what they wanted it to look like, and also what they didn't want. (For example, one of the teenagers expressed that he didn't want to be forced to pray aloud, and the seven-year-old requested the prayer meeting not be "way too long!")[1]

How to Structure Your Family Prayer

Consider designing your family prayer time in a way that best fits your family, and according to each person's ability and desire to participate. This will vary from family to family and may also evolve over time. There is no perfect starting place; you just need to take the first step. God will show up and help you!

Most families I know who pray together have shared with me that they have found a pattern that fits their lifestyle. As you create your family's unique plan, you may find these questions a helpful guide:

1. When and where will we meet?

Just like Julie and Greg did, you could call your family together and discuss the idea of devoting a particular time each day or week to come together for family worship and prayer. Find a time you can all agree on, and set it aside for family prayer, no matter what tries to interfere. Choose a place that is not only comfortable but that is also conducive to meeting with God. Start with praying over that setting and dedicating it to the Lord. Even if it's your living room, kitchen, bedroom, or patio and is used for many other purposes, reserve it as a special place where you and your family will come to meet with God. There are amazing stories both in the Bible and in modern life of how the presence of God comes and lingers in a place where people regularly encounter Him.

2. *Who is going to lead?*

This question doesn't always have a single answer. Many families have found the following interchangeable roles are helpful:

- The leader: opens and closes, sets the tone, chooses the activity if there is one, seeks input from the family for ideas

- The scheduler or organizer: helps everyone know where and when to meet

- The worship leader, if desired: plans the songs or finds online worship and praise music on any number of accessible internet sources

- The scribe: keeps notes and journals the prayer requests and answers to prayer

These roles may be combined or may change over time, especially as children grow older and become ready and interested in taking on more of a leadership role. Our friends Lance and Annabelle Wallnau, who had three young adult children still living at home at the time, shared with me how their family prayer leadership has evolved over time: "Lance and I used to be the catalyst to bring our children together for prayer, but now our oldest son is the one inviting us. Without his initiative, we probably wouldn't have family devotions so consistently. He checks everyone's schedule and pulls it all together."

3. How do we keep it going with our busy schedule?

Full calendars and countless distractions may threaten to disrupt or cancel your family prayer altar. Don't get discouraged. If you do miss a week or two, don't give up. Flexibility and persistence are the keys. Start up again as soon as you can. In our house, we turn off our cell phones, computers, and TV to minimize distractions. This helps us engage with God—to make it easier to hear His voice and enjoy His presence and one another.

4. We're all so different; how do we include everyone?

It's essential to be sensitive to your family members' ages, personalities, and interests. For example, younger children can't sit still for long. They need to be active because their attention spans are short. If you have teenagers, let them help decide what the family altar will look like. Perhaps a family member is artistic and wants to express their prayers and praises through art. Allow them to share in this way and then respond with prayer and praise. You can incorporate all kinds of creativity into your family prayer time so everyone can get involved with their gifts and interests. One family member may have had a dream or impression they want to share; this can be followed by the family praying over its meaning.

5. How can we keep track of our family's prayer needs and answers?

The best way to remember family requests and praise reports is to keep some kind of journal or notes during your family prayer times. One mom, Amanda, shared with me, "When we began to keep track of our prayer requests in a spiral-bound notebook, noting needs and the answers that came, we began seeing God move—and we saw our kids' faith increase!" Consider starting the prayer time by sharing answers to prayer. This can create expectation and increases confidence that God will answer again. When you open and share from your prayer journal, you can appreciate all the amazing things your Heavenly Father has done over time in your family. This builds your faith, and your children's faith, in God's goodness and power.

6. *How do we cultivate an atmosphere that is fresh and life-giving?*

Your family prayer altar can be a delightful, happy, interactive time, filled with enthusiasm, that the whole family looks forward to with real expectancy. One tip for families who want to keep the fire burning is to make this time simple and fun. An added benefit of having a regular family prayer and worship time together is that it offers an opportunity for being intentional about things that really matter, things like:

- cheering on and encouraging each other
- connecting and affirming one another
- creating a safe place for each family member to share their heart
- building faith and security as a family with the Lord and one another
- creating a legacy of the importance and priority of God and family

7. *What should it look like?*

Your family altar might look like praying around the coffee table, sitting out on your patio, kneeling around your child's bed at night, or taking a prayer walk around your neighborhood to pray quietly for your neighbors. Or it may look like meeting via a telephone or conference call, or by using Zoom or FaceTime. Your unique family prayer times might include prayer for such issues as health, protection, provision, direction, salvation, and relationships. And it may consist of different kinds of prayer styles, such as listening prayer, blessings, requests, thanksgiving, and spiritual warfare. Your family altar can become a place of prayerful creativity with so much to choose from!

INCORPORATING WORSHIP INTO YOUR FAMILY PRAYER TIME

Families tell me all the time that they literally feel the atmosphere in their home shift when they and their family together sing or meditate on worship songs focused on the Lord. This may include music played on an iPad, mobile device, or that you create yourself. Your family may be musical and enjoy bringing this component of live worship into your altar time.

You will discover that expressing a hunger for God's presence and pursuing Him in worship is what actually opens a heavenly window to His presence and to a personal encounter with Him. Hal and I have often experienced a heavy, even "weighty" presence of the Lord that settled in our home and remained for hours or days. This affirms the truth of God's promise, *"Draw near to God, and he will draw near to you"* (James 4:8 ESV).

As you and your family engage in the practice of unhurried waiting and worshiping the Lord, He brings a softening of your hearts toward Him and one another. There grows a new sense of harmony with each other and closeness with the Lord Himself. After coming together to worship the Lord, everyone is personally refreshed and the prayers that follow are God-inspired; the Holy Spirit breathes life and faith into them.

Brad and Nikki were a couple who experienced the life-giving, atmosphere-shifting power of worship when they pledged to take the January Christian radio challenge in their hometown of Phoenix. The challenge? Listen to only Christian music for 30 days.

However, Brad and Nikki wanted to take this challenge to another level. They pledged to each other to not only fill their home with Christian worship music but to hold family devotions every night that month. They saturated their home and family with worship music.

"Every night, after we put the baby to bed, we worshiped, prayed, and read God's Word. After this, the entire atmosphere of our home changed!" Brad declared. "But that's not all. My wife and I are youth leaders at our church. When the youth group that was meeting weekly in our home began to experience this fresh atmosphere of God, the attitude of the whole youth group changed.

"Now, they no longer want to spend all their time playing video games and on social media. They are passionate about running hard after God! All they want to do is talk about God, worship Him, read God's Word, and pray!"[2]

ADVICE FOR YOUNG FAMILIES

When children are very young, especially when there are a number of them, attention spans are short, chaos is often high, and Mommy's and Daddy's energy levels often depend on how much sleep they've all had (or not) the night before! This is a typical challenge for young families, but it doesn't mean you can't enjoy gathering for prayer. For example, Brad and Nikki, whose story we just read, needed to wait to pray together until their little one was tucked quietly into bed. During this season of life, when the children are small and the activity level is high, you need to be flexible and give yourself (and others) a lot of grace. Here are some ideas for doing that:

Set an appropriate time and place.

Choose a time that is not hurried and when everyone can be present. Don't be in bondage to a fixed time, but it will help each family member remember if it is scheduled for the same time each day. It should be a time when the littles, especially, are not prone to being overly hungry or tired. Remember, quality time spent together praying is more important than the length of time.

Remove distractions.

Turn off all media and lay the mobile devices down. Quiet is a beautiful thing! *"Be still, and know that I am God"* (Ps. 46:10 ESV).

Give the Word of God priority.

You each need your own copy of the Scriptures on paper or digital. Consider using a contemporary version and read God's promises aloud as everyone follows along. You may need to be creative with little children, keeping it simple and helping them to participate. Use Bible stories, visuals, and some godly imagination.

Talk together.

This is one thing families often fail to do in our busy, device-dominated, tech-centric world. Ask questions. Discuss what God is saying to each person. Let your children ask questions and take time to respond to them.

Pray together.

Pray for each person by name and allow each family member to voice their prayer to God. My pastor always said that you really don't know a person's heart until you hear them pray. Ask for prayer and remember to journal it when God answers!

The format of a prayer meeting is not nearly as crucial as its essence—giving everyone the opportunity to touch the heart of God, crying out with authenticity. The atmosphere of the prayer meeting may vary—loud or quiet, short or long. What matters most is that we encounter the God of the universe and welcome Him to come into our lives in a fresh way.

WAYS TO PRAY

Here are suggestions for ways to pray together and different kinds of prayer you may want to incorporate into your family prayer times:

Listening Prayer

Your family prayer times can be a place to hear God's voice when you need His wisdom, direction, and strategy. The next time your family has an important decision to make, why not gather together and ask God what He has to say about the matter? Listening and waiting on the Lord in silence, often with the open Bible in our hands, allows the Lord to speak to us by His Spirit and through His Word. (See "Decision Making" within the 10-Day Family Prayer Guide in the Appendix for guidance.)

Prayers of Blessing

Your family altar is a perfect time to pray blessings over one another. Family members might pray blessings from Scripture or a prayer from their own heart. These life-giving times can encourage children and family members to see themselves as God sees them and instill hope for the future. It can be as simple as putting your arm around your husband, wife, child, or parent, and pronouncing a simple blessing like, "I bless you with peace, encouragement, health, and confidence." You may want to get started with something spontaneous. At the next family birthday party, graduation, or other special event, gather and ask everyone to pray a blessing over the honored guest. Or, the next time you are with your kids or grandkids, ask if you can pray a blessing over them. (See Chapter 8 for more guidance on praying blessings over the children in your life.)

Prayers for Provision

One area where many of us need to trust God's faithfulness is for His provision. We can trust God to provide for us regardless of the economic conditions around us. The apostle Paul tells us, *"My God will supply every need of yours according to his riches in glory in Christ Jesus"* (Phil. 4:19 ESV). During Hal's and my 40 years of marriage and serving in ministry, we've needed to believe God for mortgage payments, school tuition, clothing, and groceries. He has always provided abundantly! It's essential for our children's future that they learn God is the source of everything they need. (For more guidance, see "Praying for Your Family's Finances" within the 10-Day Family Prayer Guide in the Appendix.)

Prayers of Protection

We can secure the borders of our home and the safety of family members through our prayers. One way to do this practically is to pray God's Word over our household. For example, Psalm 91 is a great promise of God's protection. I often read it aloud in the morning, inserting the names of my family members. (See "Psalm 91 Prayer of Protection for My Family" and "Praying for Your Children's Schools" in the Appendix for more guidance.)

I asked the Lord one day, *What should we do to protect our home?* Immediately the Holy Spirit directed my thoughts to what the Israelites did when their nation was under judgment and the firstborn male child was destined to be slain. I was led to Exodus 12:5-7, where God told the Israelites to kill an unblemished lamb, take some of the blood and put it on the doorposts of the house, and verse 13 of that same chapter, *"And when I see the blood, I will pass over you; and the plague shall not be on you to destroy you"* (NKJV).

Today our protection from destruction comes through the shed blood of Jesus, the Lamb of God, our Redeemer, when we apply His blood by faith upon the thresholds of our hearts, families, and homes. We do this by acknowledging the finished work of Jesus on the cross, His blood shed for us. Then we invite Him in and keep Him central to our lives and family (see Ps. 121:7-8). We've inherited the same promises God gave Israel, and yet an even greater covenant than that of a sacrificed lamb.

Through the blood of the Lamb, Jesus Christ, the curse will pass over us too. Your family may want to receive Holy Communion together in remembrance of the sacrifice of Jesus on the cross and acknowledge the power of His blood to shield and protect you. (For more guidance, see "Celebrating Communion as a Family" within the 10-Day Family Prayer Guide in the Appendix.)

Spiritual Warfare Prayer

There are times when we are in a spiritual battle with dark forces to secure God's purposes for our life or that of our family. We may need to boldly declare God's promises in faith. You may need to fast a meal or more. In Ephesians, Paul the apostle says, *"For we wrestle not against flesh and blood, but against principalities, against powers, against the rulers of the darkness of this world, against spiritual wickedness in high places"* (Eph. 6:12 KJV). We have an enemy, satan, who has come to *"steal, kill, and destroy"* (see John 10:10).

Revival Prayer

The family altar is a place to rekindle the flame of God's passion. As we pursue a deeper intimacy with the Lord through our communion with Him, He revives us with fresh holy fire that will blaze throughout our homes, reaching into our communities and even our nation. A family altar is that special place where we can pray for revival in our schools, churches, workplaces, communities, and country. Imagine if families all across America began to pray daily for revival in our neighborhoods and nation. I believe revival fires would be set ablaze across our land. (See "Biblical Prayers for Spiritual Awakening in Our Nation" in the Appendix for guidance.)

ACTIVATION: PLANNING YOUR FAMILY PRAYER TIME

1. Call your family together and discuss the idea of dedicating a particular time once a day or week for family prayer. Find that time you can all agree upon, and

make sure it is set aside for family prayer, no matter what else tries to interfere.

2.   Start a journal or log in which you can record the date and time of your family's requests, and be sure to document when your prayers were answered.

3.   Diligently guard the prayer time. Make a covenant with each other that this family time is sacred, refusing to allow arguing or strife to disrupt or cancel your prayer time together.

4.   Enjoy your family prayer time. Don't try to be overly religious—the goal is to make this a genuine and meaningful time with God and one another.

5.   Remember, you can build a family altar anytime and at any place. Creating a family altar is about wisely setting all the pieces in place. It may take a while, but it will come together. So be patient and don't give up. (See "A Sample Family Altar" in the Appendix for more guidance.)

LET'S PRAY

Heavenly Father, just like the disciples asked You to teach them to pray, we ask You to guide our family in prayer together. Show us how our prayers can be effective and fervent. Inspire us to come together consistently and show us how to make our family time very special, filled with Your presence. Lord, draw us into communion with You and one another, even if we're traveling or on a crazy-busy day. Help us to pray every day—together! We decree that Your fire is falling upon our lives, and our hearts will burn with fresh passion for You. Amen.

CHAPTER 8

BLESSING YOUR CHILDREN: IMPARTING LIFE-CHANGING WORDS

One day some parents brought their children to Jesus so he could lay his hands on them and pray for them. ...Jesus said, "Let the children come to me. Don't stop them! For the Kingdom of Heaven belongs to those who are like these children." And he placed his hands on their heads and blessed them (Matthew 19:13-15 NLT).

Death and life are in the power of the tongue (Proverbs 18:21 NKJV).

As we look at seeing our homes and nation transformed, one of the most important things we can do is to impart blessings of life and destiny to our children and the next generation. The Lord has a great plan for this young generation—they will take the Gospel into every sphere of influence and contend for the cultural keys to the nation, bringing reformation and revival to the land. At the same time, our enemy, satan, is actively at work, strategizing how to destroy our children.

A fierce onslaught of destructive messages is warring against the minds and hearts of our sons and daughters. Negative voices bombard them daily—words intended to wound, devalue, and tell them they do not fit in. It's nearly impossible for them to sift through these adverse comments, experiences, and thought patterns and tell themselves the truth. When we, as parents and grandparents, bless our children with affirmation, favor, hope, and encouragement, it produces life-changing results. This is something you can do when your family gathers for prayer as we discussed in Chapter 7. In addition, we can speak life-giving words over the children in our lives at any place and at any time.

Children and teens today are looking for identity, a sense of belonging, and purpose in life.

These are the very areas where the enemy is attacking them. Our children are searching for answers to who they are and why God created them. They are looking for "a family," a place to belong. Unfortunately, without an understanding of God's design for their life, they may look for "family" in all the wrong places—unhealthy relationships, violent gangs, the gay-transgender community, the drug culture, just to name a few.

"Belonging" is one of the great spiritual hungers of young people today. In this battle for our children's identity, we can give them the foundation of truth they need to combat the flaming arrows coming at them each day! And we can do this by speaking truth to them. We can do this by giving them something every child is looking for—the blessing of their mother and father.

Many of us, parents and grandparents (as well as coaches, leaders, and teachers), underestimate the power our life-giving words can have upon the children in our lives. Harvard Business School studied the correlation between team performance and the frequency of praise and criticism given to the individuals on the team. *Here's what they discovered:* The highest-performing teams received nearly six positive comments for every negative one. The medium-performing teams received almost twice as many positive comments as negative ones. But the low-performing teams received almost three negative comments for every positive one.[1]

The results of this study clearly confirm that we all need to hear more positive comments, especially from our parents and extended family. And a blessing goes even further than a positive comment. Blessings are an opportunity to open our children's hearts and spiritual eyes to their loving Heavenly Father. When we declare God's promises over them, it is life-transforming!

GIVING THE BLESSING

Some years ago, Randy and Lisa discovered that the principle of blessing ran all throughout God's Word. One afternoon, the couple gathered their six young children in their living room to speak blessings over each child. Randy admits that he was a little nervous and felt awkward at first, yet he didn't let this stop him. He told the children individually how special they were to him and their mother and to God; then he blessed each one by speaking God's heart and divine purpose over them.

"You are a mighty man of God, a warrior, a child of the King," Randy said to his son Colten. "Your name means 'man of honor,'" he spoke over his other son Logan.

115

To his daughter Jordon, "You reflect the essence of God's beauty."

And to Lauren, "Your very name means victorious one; you are that in this world."

"You are beautiful, a princess," he spoke over Khrystian. "God will use you to influence the generations to come as you are obedient to Him."

"Kameryn, your name means 'beloved, sweetheart.' You will be a great blessing to all your relationships and draw many to God's Kingdom."[2]

Each generation must bless and empower the next. We see a biblical precedent for parents blessing each of their children by laying their hands on the child's head and speaking aloud the life-giving gift of inner strength, joy, healing, and grace.

Just as Randy did in this story, we can bless the children in our lives with words of affirmation, encouragement, favor, and an extraordinary future. One way we can do this is by consistently affirming our children's God-given gifts and abilities, praying God's promises over them, such as for protection, wisdom, and well-being. (For more guidance, see "Praying for Each Person's Destiny" and "Discovering Your Spiritual Gifts" within the 10-Day Family Prayer Guide in the Appendix.)

One day, in her morning prayer time, my friend Mary Ruth Swope was lamenting the fact that she lived quite far from her grandson, Daniel. It saddened her to think she would not have the opportunity to influence his spiritual, social, emotional, and physical development the way her own maternal grandmother had inspired her. As she prayed about her dilemma, Mary Ruth began to think about how parents regularly bless their children in the Jewish culture.

She thought, *Why couldn't I begin to bless my grandson every time I speak to him on the telephone? That would be a way to transfer my personal and spiritual values to Daniel when I cannot be physically present with him.*

Immediately, Mary Ruth began to write blessings. The next time she phoned Daniel, she told him she wanted to bless him. He listened intently and then responded sweetly, "Thank you, Grandmother." Four days later, she gave Daniel a second blessing.

The third time she called him, she was ready to say goodbye when Daniel asked, "Grandmother, are you going to bless me today?"

Mary Ruth says, "My heart almost leaped out of my chest as I realized God was confirming to me how meaningful the blessings had been to my precious grandson! Now when I call, I regularly speak a blessing over Daniel, focusing on different areas of his development—personally, spiritually, physically, and emotionally."[3]

Just as Mary Ruth's blessings over Daniel made her grandson feel loved, accepted, and valued, the blessings we declare over the children in our lives can mold and shape them into the person God created them to be.

A blessing is always spoken, not just kept hidden as a desire in the heart. Words have power when they are released.

"I never realized how powerful the blessings could be," one mother said, "until I began to speak blessings over my hyperactive child. Now I see changes I never thought possible as I bless him every day with peace, self-control, and unselfish love for others."[4]

A blessing is different from a prayer. When we pray, we direct our words toward God; but in a blessing, we direct our words to an individual. When our words are aligned with God's Word and spoken in the name of Jesus, we become a channel through whom God's power can flow.

We see this in Numbers 6:23-27 (NLT), where God gave precise words for how the priests were to bless the people:

> *Tell Aaron and his sons to bless the people of Israel with this special blessing:*
>
> *"May the Lord bless you and protect you. May the Lord smile on you and be gracious to you. May the Lord show you his favor and give you his peace."*
>
> *Whenever Aaron and his sons bless the people of Israel in my name, I myself will bless them.*

GENERATIONAL BLESSINGS

God has given a life-giving plan in the Bible for imparting blessings to our children. His first act after creating Adam and Eve was to bless them and say, *"Be fruitful and increase in number; fill the earth and subdue it. Rule over the fish in the sea and the birds in the sky and over every living creature that moves on the ground"* (Gen. 1:28 NIV). Here we have the first scriptural evidence that God's blessing was intended to bring forth life from generation to generation.

The patriarchs of the Old Testament went to great lengths to impart blessings to their children, especially the father to his son. This is how the benefits of God's favor are passed on from one generation to another. Abraham blessed Isaac and Isaac blessed Jacob. Jacob blessed his twelve sons.

God first spoke His blessings over Abraham, promising, *"And I will make you a great nation, and I will bless you, and make your name great; and so you shall be a blessing; and I will bless those who bless you, and the one who curses you I will curse. And in you all the families of the earth will be blessed"* (Gen. 12:2-3 NASB).

In Mark 10:16, we are told of Jesus, *"And he took them* [the children] *up in his arms, put his hands upon them, and blessed them"* (KJV).

ARE YOUR WORDS A BLESSING OR A CURSE?

The writer of Proverbs tells us that *"death and life are in the power of the tongue"* (Prov. 18:21 KJV). In contrast to a blessing, which "empowers to prosper," a curse quite simply means "to cause to fail." This statement is worth pondering for more than a few minutes.

A few words spoken in wrath or frustration can change the destiny of a child. Words that vibrate in the air for only a few seconds can reverberate in a life as long as it lasts. Negative, hurtful words can break your child's spirit and do great damage to his or her self-esteem as well as hurt your relationship with him or her. This can create a negatively charged atmosphere in the home.

It is easy to resort to yelling at our children, especially when schedules are tight and tensions are high. It's important to remember, however, that if you shout in anger, your words go into your child's heart. Rather than producing the fruit of obedience, it can cause them to rebel. It can cause resentment and breed a lack of trust. Angry words that convey to a child that he or she is worthless or stupid can cause deep wounds that produce problems well into adulthood.

Try to be sensitive to the way your words are impacting your child. Observe your child's facial expressions. What is your child telling you through his or her eyes, voice, and actions?

Words of life often start with "*You are....*" They are statements of truth that line up with what God says about your child:

- "You are fearless."
- "You are amazing."
- "You are strong."
- "You have a sharp mind."
- "You have a great heart."
- "God made you joyful."
- "God made you bold."
- "God made you merciful."

In the context of a moment of correction when, say, your child's room is a mess (again!), instead of saying, "*You are such a slob,*" you could say, "*God made you orderly and organized; the state of your bedroom does not reflect who God made you to be.*" The first sentence may be a fact, but the second is the truth.

You could follow up the statement of truth with something like, "*God made you orderly and organized, but when you don't keep your room orderly, you are operating outside of how He made you. It's my job as your parent to train you, so I am going to help you make choices consistent with how God designed you.*"

The Word reminds us, "*Fathers* [parents], *do not provoke your children to anger...but bring them up [tenderly, with lovingkindness] in the discipline and instruction of the Lord*" (Eph. 6:4 AMP). Colossians 3:21 emphasizes the high cost of exasperating our children: "*Fathers, do not exasperate your children, so that they will not lose heart*" (NASB).

Many times, negative words and criticism toward a child is a generational pattern; we are parenting and communicating with our children the way that our parents communicated with us. If this is the case for you, start with confession of the sin of the generations, as well as your own participation in it out of habit and family culture. Ask the Lord to forgive you and fill you with His Spirit and power to change. It is possible to break old habits and patterns, and transform relationships and the atmosphere of your home to one filled with more peace and honor.

BLESSING YOUR CHILD'S POTENTIAL

Blessing children accomplishes much more than merely encouraging them in their daily lives. A couple I heard of experienced this with their son, Stephen, who was not passing in school and had failed the seventh grade the previous year. Now, he had brought home his first report card with all failing grades for his second year in the same grade.

The parents held conferences with the school officials, tried punishing Stephen, and even attempted to encourage change by offering rewards for good grades. They were careful to see that Stephen was in Sunday school and church every week. In spite of all their sincere efforts, nothing was working for them. In desperation, they appealed to their pastor for prayer. Perhaps God would do something to turn Stephen's life around.

When the pastor offered to teach them the biblical principles of blessing, they readily accepted. Soon they were applying God's Word of speaking blessings over Stephen's life, laying hands on him daily and speaking God's purpose and success into every area of his life and education. Stephen's attitudes began to change. He completed the seventh grade that year with high scores and moved into the eighth grade where he continued to succeed.

Other parents with similar cases have seen their children advance in school as they learned to speak blessings over their children's lives. Their diligence in imparting blessings has paid off for them and their children.[5]

Jesus' last act toward His disciples was to speak a blessing over them. Just before He ascended into the clouds, Jesus lifted His hands after the fashion of the priests, speaking life, peace, and success over them.

Jesus had expressed the idea of blessing to them in Matthew 5:13-14 (ESV), saying to His disciples, *"You are the salt of the earth... you are the light of the world."* At that time, His disciples were neither of those things, yet Jesus said they were. Some of them had serious character defects, which Jesus knew would take time to remedy. They were unregenerated men who would not enter into the joy of being born again until after Jesus' crucifixion and resurrection. The active speaking of that kind of success over their lives was a blessing that became a reality.

The powerful truth about blessings is this: Blessings don't depend upon the character or condition of the one receiving them. A blessing's true value is not linked to a person's performance or outward appearance. We cannot confuse the word *bless* with the word *praise*—because those who need blessing the most are often the ones who deserve praise the least.

Blessing our children is not based upon their achievements but so they can be all God wants them to be. This is the reason that we impart blessings "by faith." Hebrews tells us that "by faith" Isaac blessed Jacob and Esau, and "by faith" Jacob blessed each of Joseph's sons (see Heb. 11:20-21).

CONSEQUENCES OF WITHHOLDING BLESSINGS

Why do we withhold blessings? If the truth is known, many parents don't give the blessing to their children because they've never received it themselves. They've never seen it modeled. Perhaps the rule in your family as you were growing up was "words of love and acceptance are best kept unspoken."[6]

We have allowed a thief in our homes, robbing us of precious moments to bless our children with words of acceptance. Parents often are too distracted or tired to speak treasured words over their children and the opportunities are crowded out by busy schedules.

Earlier in this chapter, we noted that God commanded the priests to bless the people. As New Testament believers, we are all priests (see 1 Pet. 2:9). In this respect, withholding blessings goes against part of the essential nature of our purpose as Christians, the "priesthood of the believer." Withholding blessings from children can:

- cause discouragement, rejection, and offense

- create opportunities for the enemy to deceive and influence your child through perceived rejection, hurt feelings, condemnation, self-hatred, and bitterness

- dampen their desire to please their parents or serve in the home

- block the release of God's favor

- rob joy from you and your children
- create an atmosphere in the home that is spiritually and emotionally cold
- cause you to misrepresent God
- deny them the security and affirmation that they need to grow emotionally strong and healthy
- rob your family of generational blessings[7]

You may be feeling a little inadequate to bless your kids, just like Randy (the dad we mentioned earlier in the chapter) felt at first. You may not feel you have what it takes to do this. Maybe you are guilt-ridden because you don't feel you've been the best parent. Don't let this stop you from freely speaking and praying blessings over your children today. Just as a blessing is not dependent upon the condition of the one receiving it, the fulfillment of the blessing does not depend upon the one giving it.[8]

NEVER TOO EARLY OR TOO LATE

From the time our children are babies in the womb, and continuing throughout their entire lives, we can pray for, speak blessings, and instill a sense of godly purpose and destiny into them. We can help them discover their spiritual gifts and callings and prepare them to bring godly transformation into the spheres of influence to which they have been called, so they in turn will influence their own children and grandchildren through many generations. *"His offspring will be mighty in the land; the generation of the upright will be blessed"* (Ps. 112:2 ESV).

Introducing the concept of blessings into your family offers an excellent opportunity to let your kids know you've not always known what to do, that you've made some mistakes. If this is so, humbly confess it to them and bless them. You might even say to your adult children, "I wish I'd known to do this when you were younger, but I want to do this now." I've seen great healing and reconciliation come to families by this one simple act.

Life-producing words have the power to rebuild broken lives, families, and cultures. Your children may just come back to you days or years later and tell you how your spoken blessings began to unlock their hearts. When you bless your children, you set up a blessing cycle—they in turn will pass on the blessing to their children, and them to their children, and them to their children. So do not abandon your children's hearts, but bless them. Generations to come are counting on you!

ACTIVATION: BLESSING THE CHILDREN IN YOUR LIFE

1. Set aside a time to bless the children in your life individually. Use God's richest promises in the Bible to write out blessings for each one. As you bless each child, lay your hands on their head and speak aloud your life-giving words. Watch as God meets you in this act of empowerment to birth new life and joy in these most precious relationships.

2. Ask the Lord to reveal each child's natural and spiritual abilities and gifts. God endows children in the

womb with those faculties that will assist them in His calling.

3. Look for ways to bless and speak life-giving words to the children in your life regularly. The following suggestions can affect your young children's thoughts, sensibilities, habits, actions, and character development:

    ▪ Read Scriptures aloud to your baby in the womb. God's Word nourishes the unborn child's spirit and plants a love for God's Word in your baby.

    ▪ Pray for your child's salvation from the moment of conception, declaring he or she will come to know the Lord at an early age.

    ▪ Pray God's Word for your children daily. (See "Praying God's Promises for My Children" in the Appendix for more guidance.)

    ▪ Agree with what Christ says about children and speak His life-giving words aloud to your children on a regular basis. Affirm and call out their full potential in Christ often!

    ▪ Read and sing God's Word, children's lullabies, poems, and stories with Christian ideals to your young ones.

    ▪ Memorize God's promises together with your little ones.

- As your children learn to read, direct them to read God's Word daily and teach them to declare His promises over their lives.

Building these habits into your children at an early age nurtures a lifelong love of God and His Word and builds strong, healthy families.

LET'S PRAY

Dear Heavenly Father, please forgive me for the times my words have brought pain rather than healing and blessing to my child/children. I desire with my whole heart to speak life-giving words to my children and to look for creative opportunities to bless them daily. Today I bless my children with the assurance of Your love and mine. I bless them with a tender heart and sensitive spirit to hear Your voice and make the right choices. I bless my children with favor, protection, and encouragement. I bless them with good study habits, a desire to learn, and a strong memory to do well in school. I bless them with godly friends who desire to live good and moral lives. I bless them with Your highest and best teachers both spiritually and academically. I decree that my children are taught of the Lord and great is their peace and undisturbed composure (see Isa. 54:13 AMP). Amen.

PRAYER WITH THE FAMILY OF GOD: DISCOVER EXPONENTIAL RESULTS WHEN THE EKKLESIA STANDS TOGETHER

Again I say to you, that if two believers on earth agree [that is, are of one mind, in harmony] about anything that they ask [within the will of God], it will be done for them by My Father in heaven. For where two or three are gathered in My name [meeting together as My followers], I am there among them (Matthew 18:19-20 AMP).

As you continue building your family foundation, why not consider expanding your prayer altar to your brothers and sisters in the family of God? Jesus calls His Church "family," members of His household (see Eph. 2:19). In fact, when you think about it, that's what the Church is made up of—we are a community of families.

The early Church met together as family groups for more than 300 years in homes. They were a spiritual community devoted to deep, abiding relationships, prayer, and study of God's Word. In the book of Acts, we see Christ's followers exhibiting many of the characteristics of a family. *"All the believers devoted themselves to the apostles' teaching, and to fellowship, and to sharing in meals...and to prayer"* (Acts 2:42 NLT).

Jesus referred to His Church as the "called-out ones" (see Matt. 16:18). You probably know in the original Greek language the word for Church is *ekklesia*. In the days of the apostles, it did not mean a religious service, organization, or building; it was a group of people who exemplified the values and displayed the power of God and influenced their community.

When families operated as a praying community in their role as the *ekklesia*, they experienced powerful synergy and increased authority over the darkness trying to capture their families and nation. These praying groups of families became the catalyst for some significant moves of God. One of these was the one that started in the "upper room." This is the earliest account we have of believers coming together after Jesus' crucifixion, resurrection, and ascension to Heaven.

They were staying there, in Jerusalem, seeking God together with one heart, praying daily and kindling their passion for God to fulfill the Joel 2:28-32 promise spoken to them by Jesus. At this "prayer altar," they pursued God to empower them to accomplish all He had commanded them to do. It might be easy to miss that these were families that gathered: Mary the mother of Jesus and Jesus' brothers, the disciples, and certain women (wives and sisters) as well (see Acts 1:14). The "upper room" was a familiar place where presumably prayer meetings were held regularly.

These 120 friends and family of Jesus knew they likely would suffer the same fate as their Leader—persecution, prison, and even crucifixion by the religious and Roman leaders. They longed for courage and strength to obey their Master. Remembering the words of Jesus Himself who instructed them to gather and wait until they were *"clothed with power from on high,"* they gathered in the *"upper room"* (see Luke 24:49; Acts 1:8,13).

When the Spirit came, He manifested His Presence as "tongues of fire" from Heaven, falling upon the families who were in that place. These flames on the altar of their prayers were a demonstration that, just as Jesus promised, they would be clothed with power and strength: *"And when they had prayed, the place in which they were assembled was shaken: and they were all filled with the Holy Spirit, and they continued to speak the Word of God with freedom and boldness and courage"* (Acts 4:31 AMPC).

This newly empowered *ekklesia*, who moments earlier were frightened, weak, and insecure believers, were now baptized with courage and strength of the "Holy Spirit and fire."[1] The Holy Spirit transformed them into a spiritual powerhouse.[2] They did not stay within "the four walls" of a church. They were out in the streets—they raised the dead, healed the sick, cast out demons, and preached with such authority and boldness that thousands became believers in Jesus, entering into God's Kingdom daily.[3]

PRAYING IN ONE ACCORD

The Acts Church was not deceived. They did not see an "imbalance" in their engaging in prayer together so much of the time. Acts 2:46 (KJV) says they were *"continuing daily with one accord in the temple."* Peter and John were on their way to a prayer meeting when they healed the lame man (see Acts 3)—a prayer meeting where *"they lifted up their voices to God with one accord,"* producing a literal shaking of the house in which they prayed (see Acts 4:24-31 BSB). Peter was miraculously delivered from prison through the prayers of the saints gathered in a home. In all these instances the Lord released exponential power when they prayed together as the *ekklesia* (see Matt. 18:19)!

Pastor Jim Cymbala, of the famed Brooklyn Tabernacle in New York City, shares this story about the power of praying in one accord with the family of God in his book *Fresh Wind, Fresh Fire*:

> Our oldest daughter, Chrissy, was a model child growing up. But around age sixteen, she started to stray. I admit I was slow to notice this—I was too occupied with the church, starting branch congregations, overseeing projects, and all the rest that ministry entails.
>
> Meanwhile, Chrissy not only drew away from us but also away from God. In time, she even left our home. There were many nights when we had no idea where she was.
>
> As the situation grew more serious, I tried everything. I begged, I pleaded, I scolded, I argued, I tried to control her with money. Looking back, I recognize the foolishness of my actions. Nothing worked; she just hardened more and more.
>
> ...Eventually, there came a divine showdown. God strongly impressed me to stop crying, screaming, or talking to anyone else about Chrissy. I was to converse with no one but God. In fact, I knew I should have no further contact with Chrissy—until God acted! I was

just to believe and obey what I had preached so often: Call upon me in the day of trouble, and I will answer you.

...I began to pray with an intensity and growing faith as never before. Whatever bad news I would receive about Chrissy, I kept interceding and actually began praising God for what I knew He would do soon. I made no attempts to see her. (My wife) Carol and I endured that Christmas season with real sadness.

February came. One cold Tuesday night during the prayer meeting, I talked from Acts 4 about the church boldly calling on God in the face of persecution. We entered into a time of prayer, everyone reaching out to the Lord simultaneously.

An usher handed me a note. A young woman I felt to be spiritually sensitive had written: "Pastor Cymbala, I feel impressed that we should stop the meeting and all pray for your daughter."

I hesitated. Was it right to change the flow of the service and focus on my personal need?

Yet something in the note seemed to ring true. In a few minutes, I picked up the microphone and told the congregation what had just happened. "The truth of the matter," I said, "although I haven't talked much about it, is that my daughter is very far from God these days. She thinks that up is down and down is up; dark is light, and light is dark. But I know God can break through to her, and so I'm going to ask Pastor Boekstaaf to lead us in praying for Chrissy. Let's all join hands across the sanctuary."

To describe what happened in the next minutes, I can only employ a metaphor: the church turned into a labor room.

...There arose a groaning, a sense of desperate determination, as if to say, "Satan, you will not have this girl. Take your hands off her—she's coming back!" I was overwhelmed. The force of that vast throng, calling on God, almost literally knocked me over.

When I got home that night, Carol was waiting up for me. We sat at the kitchen table drinking coffee, and I said, "It's over."

"What's over?" she wondered.

"It's over with Chrissy. You would've had to be in the prayer meeting tonight. I tell you, if there's a God in Heaven, this whole nightmare is finally over."

Thirty-two hours later, on Thursday morning, as I was shaving, Carol suddenly burst through the door, her eyes wide. "Go downstairs!" she blurted. "Chrissy's here."

"Chrissy is here?"

"Yes! Go down!"

"But Carol—I—"

"Just go down," she urged. "It's you she wants to see."

I wiped off the shaving foam and headed down the stairs, my heart pounding. As I came around the corner, I saw my daughter on the kitchen floor...sobbing. Cautiously I spoke her name:

"Chrissy?"

She grabbed my pant leg and began pouring out her anguish. "Daddy—Daddy—I've sinned against God. I've sinned against myself. I've sinned against you and Mommy. Please forgive me."

My vision was as clouded by tears as hers. I pulled her up from the floor and held her close...

Suddenly she drew back. "Daddy," she said with a start, "who was praying for me? Who was praying for me?" Her voice was like that of a cross-examining attorney.

"What do you mean, Chrissy?"

"On Tuesday night, Daddy—who was praying for me?"

I didn't say anything, so she continued:

"In the middle of the night, God woke me and showed me I was heading toward this abyss. There was no bottom to it—it scared me to death. I was so frightened. I realized how hard I've been, how wrong, how rebellious.

"But at the same time, it was like God wrapped His arms around me and held me tight. He kept me from sliding any further as He said, 'I still love you.'

"Daddy, tell me the truth—who was praying for me Tuesday night?"

I looked into her bloodshot eyes, and once again I recognized the daughter we had raised.

Chrissy's return to the Lord became evident immediately. By that fall, God had opened a miraculous door for her to enroll at a Bible college, where she not only undertook studies but soon began directing music groups and a large choir, just like her mother. Today she is a pastor's wife in the Midwest with three wonderful children.[4] (See "Praying for Loved Ones to Know Christ" in the Appendix for more guidance in how to pray for your own family.)

In times like these, as the Cymbalas experienced, we, as believers in Jesus, need to gather as the *ekklesia* and take advantage of the unlimited faith, strength, courage, and authority that the prayers of the Body of Christ can accomplish. Corporately, we activate the power of agreement that Jesus promised us when He said:

> *Truly, I say to you, whatever you bind on earth shall be bound in heaven, and whatever you loose on earth shall be loosed in heaven. Again I say to you, if two of you agree on earth about anything they ask, it will be done for them by my Father in heaven. For where two or three are gathered in my name, there am I among them* (Matthew 18:18-20 ESV).

I believe one of the great shifts in process within the Body of Christ right now is regarding our role to operate at a high level as His *ekklesia*—a "house of prayer," understanding our authority in binding and loosing, opening and closing spiritual doors, and releasing Heaven's decrees as representatives of Christ's Kingdom on earth.

My friend Germaine Copeland has been experiencing this for many years. She wrote her best-selling book, *Prayers That Avail Much,* from the testimonies of those who attended the weekly prayer meeting she held in her home. Women gathered to pray fervently in agreement for one another's families, including some of the direst circumstances imaginable.

Thankfully, they had the forethought to keep a journal of prayer requests and the astounding answers to prayer so that we can glean from those prayers today. Noting how a two-hour once-a-week prayer meeting could bring so many miraculous results, Germaine captured those stories in her books. She has inspired millions to experience the exponential power released when we pray *together*.

I liken this phenomenon to how a mighty fire can be built. Each of us in the family of God is like a burning coal. When we come together in prayer, we ignite one another until corporately we become like an enormous, burning furnace! (If you'd like to start a prayer meeting in your home as Germaine did, see "Tips for Leading a Small-Group Prayer Meeting" in the Appendix.)

HISTORICAL PRAYER MOVEMENTS THAT RELEASED GOD'S POWER

I love reading historical accounts of how God powerfully uses His Church, the *ekklesia*, worldwide when we are united in prayer and Kingdom authority and producing exponential results.

One group of believers that famously experienced this is the Moravians in Europe in the 1700s. Fleeing religious persecution in their home country of Moravia, they established the village of Herrnhut in Germany in 1722. (*Herrnhut* means "the Lord's watch.") Count Nikolaus Ludwig von Zinzendorf, who owned the land on which they built their village, was only 22 years old at the time he granted them asylum.

Soon afterward, he formed a group called the "band of four brothers" with three of his friends. They frequently met for prayer and Bible study and proceeded to stir up a small regional revival. They printed and distributed large quantities of Bibles, books, tracts, and collections of hymns. After the group's establishment, Zinzendorf moved to Herrnhut with his wife and children.

Life was not all peaceful, however. Once the Moravians had escaped the external pressures of their previous home, strife and division began to tear at them from within. They carried deep wounds from their persecution and seemed to argue about everything.

Zinzendorf, being a man of God, would not stand for this infighting. Finally, on May 12, 1727, the community reached a turning point when Zinzendorf gave a three-hour address on the blessedness of Christian unity. The entire congregation responded with repentance, and a revival swept the village.

That summer of 1727 was a golden one for the Moravian community, whose hearts were again being knit together by the Holy Spirit. But the Lord was just getting started. In early August, Zinzendorf and 14 other Moravian brethren spent a night in conversation and prayer. A short time later on August 13, the community experienced a day of the outpouring of the Holy Spirit upon the congregation; it was its "Pentecost." It was an experience that would change the Moravians and the world!

The Moravians didn't only experience revival that summer; revival became a permanent part of their community's culture and governance. Before the end of that month, 24 men and 24 women pledged to pray for one hour a day in turn, for every hour of the day, seven days a week. This "hourly intercession" continued nonstop for the next 100 years!

One of the governing Scriptures God gave them during this time is found in Leviticus 6:13 (NKJV): *"A fire shall always be burning on the altar; it shall never go out."* As they obeyed God's Word, the Moravians grew together to become a community like none the world had ever seen before. It was undoubtedly their version of God's "city on a hill" from which His light would shine worldwide. The Moravians were among the first Protestants to leave Europe to take God's Word to unreached ethnic groups. Everything the Moravians did began with prayer, was bathed in prayer, and was carried out in prayer. The Gospel they took into the world brought reformation, and many nations bound in darkness have been touched as a result of the missionary movement begun by the Moravians.[5]

Three principles guided everything the Moravians did. James Goll writes about these in his book *The Lost Art of Intercession*:

1. They had relational unity, spiritual community, and sacrificial living.

2. The power of their persistent prayer produced a divine passion and zeal for missionary outreach to the lost.

3. They lived by the motto: "No one works unless someone prays," and made a corporate commitment to sustained prayer and ministry to the Lord.[6]

THE HAYSTACK REVIVAL

Here is another really encouraging story of when five young college students decided they would pray together, and it started a whole movement!

The five young men, calling themselves "the Brethren," were students at Williams College in Massachusetts in 1806. They experienced hostility toward Christians on their campus that was so intense that they were afraid to let anyone know they were praying, and even kept the minutes of their meetings hidden. So, they went off campus to a nearby farm to pray for revival for their school.

As they were praying and discussing revival and the theology of missionary service in a grove of trees near the Hoosac River, a severe thunderstorm broke out. For protection, they sought refuge under a haystack in a nearby barn, where they continued to intercede! That "Haystack Prayer Meeting" sparked a revival on the campus of Williams College, and not long afterward, a powerful world-wide missions movement from America. All from five kids praying in a haystack!

BUSINESSMEN SPARK A REVIVAL THROUGH PRAYER

I'm always amazed how such great revivals break out as a result of the faith and obedience of a small group of ordinary individuals who gather to pray. A favorite of mine is the story of Jeremiah Lanphier and the small prayer meeting he started for businessmen in New York City.

On September 23, 1857, the United States was in spiritual, political, and economic decline. America desperately needed prayer. Many people were disillusioned with spiritual things as well as the downward spiral of the American economy.

Lanphier had posted a sign on the Fulton Street Church building that read: *Prayer meeting from 12 to 1 o'clock—Stop 5, 10, or 20 minutes, or the whole hour, as your time permits.* Jeremiah waited ten minutes, then ten more. By 12:30, no one had come. Then at 12:30, one man entered the room, followed by another and another until finally six men were praying. Nothing extraordinary happened that hour, but the men decided to meet to pray the following week.

That time 20 men came; the next week, 40. Because of the climbing interest in prayer, Jeremiah decided they should meet for prayer daily. Within days of that decision, a financial panic hit the country. Banks began to close and people lost their jobs. Conditions were ripe for a revival. Soon, 3,000 people were jamming into the Fulton building to pray. Within six months 20,000 pray-ers came, and at least 20 other corporate meetings had begun in the city. Corporate prayer movements such as these began to spread quickly across the nation and in different parts of the world.

Business people led the meetings, not church leaders, and prayer was the focus rather than preaching. The gatherings themselves were informal—any person might pray, lead in a hymn, or give a word of testimony, with a five-minute limit placed on each participant.

The years 1858-59 became known as the *Annus Mirabilis*—Year of Miracles. During this era, great leaders such as Dwight Moody, Andrew Murray, and William Booth were launched into ministry, and a great missionary movement was birthed. When Jeremiah and his five prayer partners began their prayer vigil, they had no idea that God would bring an estimated one million people into His Kingdom through their efforts.

The Fulton Street prayer meeting is just one of thousands of examples of multitudes coming to Christ during Great Awakenings ignited by corporate prayer.[7] These stories inspire me about what God can do with a small band of praying believers. He simply is looking for a few committed people He can use to accomplish great things. Across time, the prayers of the *ekklesia* have produced powerful results—like the early Church, the praying Moravians, the haystack students, Jeremiah Lanphier and his small downtown prayer meeting, and many more. God uses these kinds of prayer altars to occupy territory, advance His Kingdom, break the powers of darkness, and invite His redeeming presence. This strategy of creating prayer altars within the family of God, taken straight from the Word of God, has ignited revival in entire nations. And the best part of this is, God is still using this strategy for revival today.

ACTIVATION: EXPANDING YOUR FAMILY PRAYER CIRCLE

1. Consider inviting another family to your home for a meal followed by a time of prayer. Perhaps this would be someone who is going through a difficult time or has a significant need. Or invite some friends who have mutual concerns for revival in your community and nation. You also can always pray for each other's children and families, marriages, workplace, etc.

2. If that's not an option for you right now, enlist a prayer partner (or two or three) who might meet with you at a park, a coffee shop with a private room, or one of your homes.

3. Take some time in advance to pray for the people you'll be joining with; invite the Holy Spirit to be present in your prayer time, and ask Him to guide your prayers to be highly effectual, with powerful results (see James 5:16). It's essential to find someone outside your own household and a part of the family

of God with whom you can join forces and pray together in agreement as His ekklesia.

LET'S PRAY

Thank You, Lord, for the gift of family, and that we can be part of the family of God. Thank You for the privilege of coming together in agreement with the assurance that when we cry out to You, according to Your Word, You will answer. We ask forgiveness for failing to live together as Your ekklesia, Your called-out ones, and for not walking in the unity and authority You have called us to exercise together. We make a fresh commitment to reach out to others in the Body of Christ—to pray with them and for them, and to intercede together for the needs of our community and nation. We decree that the family of God is coming together in united, fervent prayer, prodigals are coming home, massive numbers of people are coming to Christ, and another Great Awakening is breaking forth in our nation. Amen.

PART THREE

SHIFTING THE SPIRITUAL CLIMATE—DRAWING THE PRESENCE OF GOD

CHAPTER 10

How to Create a Life-Giving Atmosphere in Your Home: Living Under an Open Heaven

The Lord will open the heavens, the storehouse of his bounty, to send rain on your land in season and to bless all the work of your hands (Deuteronomy 28:12 NIV).

I am sure you have felt it. You walk into a store or someone's home and immediately feel something difficult to explain, whether it is peace and joy or a prevailing darkness and heaviness. Every household, workplace, neighborhood, and even nation has a unique spiritual atmosphere or prevalent climate.

Yet most of us would say it is the atmosphere in our home that impacts us more than anywhere else. The whole world looks brighter when everyone is getting along, loving God and one other. In these

147

times when the "climate" of our family is warm and faith-filled, our family members will likely be content, confident, and connected.

On the other hand, when we allow life's challenges to harden our hearts, it opens the door for the atmosphere of our home to turn hostile, distant, or selfish. When this happens, we generally experience a corresponding atmosphere of unhappiness and conflict.

What is the atmosphere like in your home? Think about it for a moment. Then imagine what it would be like if the atmosphere of your home was more inviting and Spirit-filled. What if you could experience a supernatural atmosphere, one alive with God's presence, God's voice, and God's promises? What if you could experience the atmosphere of Heaven in *your* home?

You might be thinking, "This is not possible!" However, Jesus told us to pray this way: *"Your kingdom come, your will be done, on earth as it is in heaven"* (Matt. 6:10 NIV). Why would Jesus have told us to pray for something that was not possible to attain? Simply stated, Jesus asked us to pray that Heaven would come to earth because that is His perfect will.

HEAVEN IN YOUR HOME

In my book *Prayer-Saturated Kids*, I tell about a time when Heaven came down and touched our home, and I mean this literally. When Nicole was a little girl, Hal was often away on mission trips. During these times, especially at night, Nicole felt unsettled. She missed her dad and the sense of safety he brought to our home. On several occasions, Nicole lay awake the entire night, crying and fearful. The following morning, she would be so worn out that I would have to keep her home from preschool. So, when Hal discovered he would be taking a two-week trip to the Philippines, we were concerned about the trip's effect on Nicole.

During those early days, our family altar most often took place each night around Nicole's bed. We worshiped the Lord together, we prayed for Nicole, and then she would pray for her friends and the things that were on her heart. The night before Hal left on his trip, we gathered in Nicole's room and knelt beside her bed. Hal talked about God's protection and the work of guardian angels. Then he prayed over her and read from Scripture: *"He will give His angels [especial] charge over you to accompany and defend and preserve you in all your ways [of obedience and service]"* (Ps. 91:11 AMPC). We took authority over the fear that was attacking our daughter and prayed she would have absolute assurance that her Heavenly Father was watching over her.

The next morning after Hal left for the Philippines, Nicole awoke and told me that something spectacular had happened during the night. "The angels came last night, Mommy!" she exclaimed.

"Oh?" I questioned. "Tell me more. What happened?"

"They were standing in a circle around my bed, singing. And, oh, it was the most beautiful singing I've ever heard!"

"What did they look like?" I asked.

Without the slightest hesitation, Nicole shared in detail what she had seen. "Some were so tall their heads touched the ceiling, and some were little, *like me*. Some had on gold sandals, and some had on gold belts. And they were *so* white and *so* bright, Mommy!"

Had I not had a similar experience some 15 years earlier, I might have been tempted to dismiss Nicole's experience as childish imagination. At a time in my life when I felt frightened and all alone, I awoke to find a huge angelic being standing over me. He was so tall his head touched the ceiling, and his wings were the whitest white I had ever seen. The light was so bright I could not keep my eyes open! The presence of the Lord permeated my being, and I felt a powerful sense of God's peace and protection.

Nicole never again cried about her dad being away or mentioned being fearful because of his absence. This was concrete evidence that when Hal and I prayed God's Word and asked the Lord to send His angels to protect Nicole, this was more than symbolic—He actually did it! When we exercised our spiritual authority in prayer, we shut fear out of our home and invited God's tangible protection and presence to dwell there!

Yes, it truly is possible for the tangible atmosphere of Heaven to touch earth, especially in our homes.

THE TWO REALMS

The Bible tells us that our world has two realms—a physical realm and an invisible spiritual realm. Just because we cannot see or often perceive the spiritual realm doesn't make it any less real. It influences our lives—and the atmosphere in our homes—more than we may realize. It affects the mind, will, and emotions of everyone who lives there. A spiritual atmosphere, good or evil, has the power to shape our lives—to inspire or confuse, to affirm or reject, to make happy or sad, to empower or restrict.

How can you tell which atmosphere is influencing your home? Take a look at Scripture: *"The kingdom of God is...righteousness, peace and joy in the Holy Spirit"* (Rom. 14:17 NIV). In other words, when God's Spirit is welcome in your home, you can expect to experience an atmosphere of peace and joy that will influence everyone who dwells there. That is an incredible promise!

On the other hand, the Bible tells us that we have a spiritual enemy who comes to *"steal and kill and destroy"* (John 10:10 ESV). When these dark forces work in our homes, they rob our peace, finances, and health. They are bent on destroying our family's joy and unity.[1]

We may feel powerless to change a hostile atmosphere and think, *That's just the way things are!* But that's simply not true. Storms can be calmed instantly, as the disciples witnessed when Jesus rebuked a turbulent storm at sea (see Matt. 8:23-27). It's true of a stormy spiritual climate as well.

THE BATTLE OF TWO FORCES

In the layers of our atmosphere surrounding the earth, there are negatively and positively charged ions. Our homes, too, can harbor a negatively charged atmosphere empowered by evil forces or a positively charged atmosphere that finds its source in God, His Word, and His Holy Spirit.

A negatively charged atmosphere is characterized by:

- defeatism and lack of purpose or vision for the future
- confusion, chaos, and disorder
- acceptance of demonic activity
- control, dominance, or haughtiness
- weariness and hopelessness
- a bankrupt spirit or a mindset of lack or scarcity
- spiritual and emotional distance
- hurt feelings and holding resentments

- selfishness or rebellion
- pride or a condescending attitude
- bitterness, anger, and cynicism
- insecurity, fear, or anxiety
- lack of spiritual life or momentum
- impurity, irreverence, or vulgarity
- pervasive and persistent illnesses

A positively charged atmosphere is characterized by:

- hope and vision for the future
- a sense of order that produces peace
- atmosphere of an "open heaven" (God's supernatural power is both felt and seen)
- liberty and freedom
- confidence and expectancy in God—that nothing is impossible, no problem is too big for Him
- God's faithful financial provision and blessing
- trust, connection, warmth, and mutual support
- compassion, forgiveness, and patience
- respect, honor, and integrity
- value and significance of everyone
- unity, harmony, and encouragement
- triumphant outlook with strength and endurance
- alive with God's presence, voice, and promises

- God-honoring and pure spirit

- health, healing, and wholeness

So, how do we dispel the darkness from our homes? How do we welcome the Holy Spirit's presence and power?

YOU HAVE AUTHORITY TO CHANGE THE ATMOSPHERE

Dutch Sheets is a best-selling author, speaker, and former pastor. He shares this story about authority in prayer to change the atmosphere in your home:

> When the Lord first started talking to me about changing the atmosphere, He started by dealing with me about the atmosphere in my home. One morning in our house, there was this tension. We have a great family relationship—all of us. We don't fight, and my wife, Ceci, and I don't argue. We talk things through. We make sure we honor one another in that way. But everybody was kind of on edge, irritated and frustrated. Nobody had a reason. So, everybody had to guard their tongue and be careful. Finally, I just said—sort of to myself—*Lord, I really don't like the atmosphere in here right now.*
>
> Just as clearly as I have ever heard the Lord, He said, "Well, why don't you change it?" The Lord said, "You're in charge of your house. You have authority here. Just begin to decree My Word and decree that the tension has to leave, and the peace of God will fill the atmosphere of your house."

I thought, *I'm going to try this and see what happens.* I didn't gather the family and pray because I didn't want them to know what I was doing. I wanted to know whether this was going to be something supernatural or people just trying harder. For only five minutes, I walked through the house and, under my breath, I quietly started praying and decreeing. Within minutes—not hours, but minutes—the atmosphere changed. People were singing and happy, and engaging one another in conversation. It was like they'd had their morning cup of coffee—everybody changed. I thought, *Wow, this is pretty good.*

Dutch gives us a powerful and practical model here that we can apply. Every day we are in various spiritual battles relating to our families, workplaces, and communities. However, in the end, we must remember that *the war is over the presence of God.* Who will rule the atmosphere in a given place? Will it be the Holy Spirit or something else?

Hal and I have had similar experiences. Once, I was thinking of canceling our family vacation. It was not because I didn't want to go and not because we didn't desperately need to get away. We hadn't had a real vacation in over five years.

I just didn't feel getting away was going to help our situation. I was exhausted. And, quite honestly, I was angry that the best we could do was carve out three days away when what we really needed was three weeks!

We'd been working long hours and managing the stress of limited income in the ministry. Whenever I walked into my house, all I noticed was the worn carpet, old fixtures, and the leaking shower.

Admittedly my prayer times were dry, and I knew I wasn't connecting well with the Lord—or with Hal! The glass I was holding in my hand didn't look half full—it was nearly empty.

So, when our good friends offered us their beautiful home on the beach in Rocky Point, Mexico, we accepted. Staying home wasn't going to be a better option.

When I woke up on the first morning at the beach house, I could see the beautiful sandy beach and blue glistening water outside my bedroom window. Hal had awakened earlier and was already upstairs taking in the view. But for me, I couldn't seem to enjoy it. A dark cloud of depression blanketed me. Instantly, the Holy Spirit showed me the heaviness hanging over me was because of the anger and unforgiveness I was unknowingly harboring toward Hal and toward the Lord.

"God, I'm so sorry," I prayed. "I've gotten so busy that I've forgotten to thank You for all You've done for my family and me. For all You've given me, my wonderful husband, our daughter, and for the way You've protected our whole family. I'm so sorry for being angry and ungrateful. Please forgive me."

Instantly I felt something like a spiritual washing come over my whole being. I lifted my hands to the Lord, welcoming Him into my heart and the home where we were staying. I prayed, "This new day I invite the very atmosphere of Heaven, the glory of God, into my life, into my marriage, my family, and this weekend at Rocky Point." Then I boldly told the dark forces plaguing me that my family and I were off-limits.

I knew something had changed.

When I went upstairs, I told Hal what had happened, and we turned our hearts to the Lord and each other with fresh expectation.

We didn't try to make anything happen; we just let God unfold His plans each day. In the afternoons, we sat on the balcony for hours listening to Spirit-filled worship music and soaking up the sights and sounds of the ocean. As wave after wave splashed upon the beach, powerful tsunami-like waves of God's Spirit saturated us. Our minds, bodies, emotions, and spirits were being brought back to life.

We worshiped, we prayed, we laughed, and we played. And we couldn't stop talking about the majesty, power, and goodness of God.

Driving home, we reminisced about the weekend; we couldn't believe what a difference three short days had made. We were experiencing the reality of God's Word, *"Now the Lord is the Spirit, and where the Spirit of the Lord is, there is freedom"* (2 Cor. 3:17 NIV).

Sunday night, when we walked into our house, nothing had changed, yet everything had changed. I didn't notice the carpet or things that needed fixing. I was overwhelmed with a spirit of gratefulness. I thanked God that I had a roof over my head, that I had a bed to sleep in at night, a hot shower, and food to eat. I thanked Him for providing all our furniture and clothing. I knew He would provide for all our other needs as well. The glass I was holding in my hand was not just full; it was running over.

Just like Dutch discovered how the power of a believer's decreeing authority in Christ overcomes the spirit of heaviness, Hal and I rediscovered that the power of forgiveness and gratitude also opens up the heavens and allows us to experience His grace, mercy, and glory. Conversely, if we hang on to our unforgiveness, we will continue to experience a hostile or depressive spiritual atmosphere—a "closed heaven." Jesus may have been alluding to this principle when He said:

> *And whenever you stand praying, if you have anything against anyone, forgive him and let it drop (leave it, let it go), in order that your Father Who is in heaven may also forgive you your [own] failings and shortcomings and let them drop. But if you do not forgive, neither will your Father in heaven forgive your failings and shortcomings* (Mark 11:25-26 AMPC).

We see a similar promise made by the apostle Paul, with a reminder that the Lord is always near; whether we experience His peace and presence or not depends much on our heart attitude, as Paul reminds us to keep an attitude of trust and thanksgiving:

> *Let your gentleness be evident to all. The Lord is near. Do not be anxious about anything, but in every situation, by prayer and petition, with thanksgiving, present your requests to God. And the peace of God, which transcends all understanding, will guard your hearts and your minds in Christ Jesus* (Philippians 4:5-7 NIV).

Whether you're meeting with God alone or as a family, ask Him to show you how to break through the darkness, encounter the presence of God, and come into communion with Him. When this happens daily, we create an atmosphere that we and everyone in our family desire to live in. Our homes become an altar to the Lord, a place of worship, prayer, and sacrificial service that attracts the presence and power of God.

What are the spiritual keys the Lord has given us to open the heavens?

- Forgiveness: releasing and letting go of offenses and hurts (see Matt. 6:14-15; Eph. 4:31-32; Col. 3:13; 1 John 1:9)

- Repentance: changing our hearts and minds and turning away from those things that do not line up with God's truth (see Prov. 28:13; Acts 3:19; Rom. 12:2; 2 Pet. 3:9)

- Worship: giving honor and adoration to God our Father and Christ Jesus, our Lord (see Ps. 95:6; Luke 4:8; Col. 3:16-17)

- Thanksgiving: remembering and thanking God for all He has done for us (see Ps. 100:4; 107:1; Eph. 5:20)

- Prayer: asking God to intervene and provide for all the concerns in our lives (see John 15:7; Phil. 4:6; 1 Thess. 5:17)

- Generosity: faithful tithing, sacrificial giving, sharing all we have in obedience to the Lord (see Mal. 3:10; Luke 6:38; 2 Cor. 9:6-8)

- Warfare: declaring God's Word over our situation as the truth. Closing the door to satan's influence over our life and family (see 2 Cor. 10:4-5)

This last point—warfare—is one that many believers fail to address in their daily lives. You need to remember you are at *war!* Two kingdoms are clashing for dominance in your life and family.

Jesus Himself was not exempt from warfare. He was "tempted by the devil" in the wilderness and given attractive opportunities. Three times Jesus was offered everything the world had to deliver, but each time He boldly told the devil to get lost: *"Away from me, Satan!"* (Matt. 4:10 NIV).

Jesus dealt fully with satan's authority at the Cross of Calvary, stripping the devil of the right to use his power and abilities against us (see Col. 2:15). Be assured, he will trespass and attempt to steal, kill, and destroy our lives, families, and happiness. We must exercise our authority over the devil's works and power just like Jesus did—with the *truth* of God's Word. The Word is the truth that sets us free from the lies and deceptions of the devil and dispels the darkness he tries to bring (see John 8:31-32, 36; Rom. 8:1-2; Gal. 5:1). When we do, God's incredible power will back up our authority and His Word.

Jesus put it this way: *"Behold, I give you the authority to trample on serpents and scorpions, and over all the power of the enemy, and nothing shall by any means hurt you"* (Luke 10:19 NKJV). This means that we don't have to submit to hostile circumstances and environments in our lives and family; we can change the atmosphere in our homes or wherever we go by walking in our God-given authority.

ACTIVATION: ASSESSING THE SPIRITUAL ATMOSPHERE IN YOUR HOME

1. Let's do an assessment. Look again at the negative and positive spiritual atmospheres listed earlier in this chapter.

2. Think about which characteristics most describe the atmosphere in your home. Write these down in your prayer journal. They point to the areas that need your attention in prayer and spiritual authority.

3. Pray and ask the Lord to help everyone to let go of all negative words and attitudes and intentionally embrace forgiveness and godly traits. You may want to write a family covenant. This is a guiding document of how the family will live and relate to one another and is to be signed willingly by parents and children. (See "Writing a Family Covenant" in the Appendix for more guidance.)

4. Invite and welcome the Holy Spirit to saturate your home with the atmosphere of Heaven—peace, joy, and righteousness! One way to do this is with God-honoring worship music and prayer.

LET'S PRAY

Thank You, Lord, that You did not leave us powerless but, in fact, have given us spiritual weapons and authority to use in Your powerful name. We thank You, Lord, that the works of darkness have no influence or authority to afflict us or prevail against us or our family. Instead, we declare that we and our household will walk in abundant life and victory because of Jesus' life, death on the cross, and resurrection from the grave! You have given us total victory over all the works of the evil one.

As believers in Jesus Christ and in Your mighty, victorious name, we decree that satan will not kill, steal, or destroy our marriage, children, health, or provision—that he will not rule the atmosphere of our home, school, workplace, or nation! We proclaim that we will live in victory and in an atmosphere of peace, joy, and righteousness in the Holy Spirit! Amen.

CHAPTER 11

IGNITING REVIVAL:
THE DIFFERENCE YOUR
PRAYER ALTAR MAKES

"Arise, walk through the length and the breadth of the land, for I will give it to you." So Abram moved his tent and came and settled by the oaks of Mamre...and there he built an altar to the Lord (Genesis 13:17-18 ESV).

We all are seeing the rise of darkness in the nations, sensing a desperate desire for God to move, and experiencing a strong need to cry out in prayer. Many of us—as leaders, parents, and intercessors—are aware that if we do not see a move of God, the devastation and consequences are unfathomable. We know that things cannot continue down the path they are going now. We must have a sustaining, transforming revival.

In the opening chapter of this book, I shared with you a prophetic word the Lord gave me concerning my nation. I was shocked; I simply could not believe that what He was saying was true. The words resounded loudly in my spirit and almost knocked me off my feet: *"Revival will come to America when the family altar is restored!"* It did not seem possible!

Then the Lord showed me a vision of the nation covered in deep darkness. As I peered into the dark sky, I saw homes begin to light up where families were praying and worshiping God together. This light exploded and spread like fire until the entire nation was ablaze with the Holy Spirit's presence and power.

CAN FAMILY PRAYER AND WORSHIP REALLY CHANGE A NATION?

Over the years I've come to a deeper understanding of what the Lord said to me concerning my nation—how His presence and influence in the home is the key to restoring and transforming a nation. My revelation of a prayer altar and its impact has grown.

As we study history, we see that the downfall of any nation always begins with the decline of the family. But consider that the family's disintegration begins when the God of the Bible is absent from family life, and worship and prayer cease to be a priority in the home.[1] This is quite profound. I want to be sure you don't miss this!

Think of it this way—if nations are made up of different people groups, and people groups are made up of families, then it is families that constitute a nation. The condition of any nation is simply a reflection of the condition of the family.

Every complex problem a nation faces can be boiled down to this: if the God of the Bible is not followed, honored, and revered in the home, the foundations of the home will crumble, and so goes the nation.

In America, Christianity is in decline, having fallen 12 percent in the last decade. Today, 63 percent of the nation calls themselves Christians.[2] But only 6 percent of Americans have a biblical worldview.[3] And sadly, less than one-half of 1 percent of Christians between the ages of 18 and 23 have a biblical worldview.[4]

As we look for the root of the problem, renowned American researcher George Barna takes us right back to the home. He says it is "Parents, to whom the Bible assigns the primary responsibility for shaping the worldview of their children," which he says begins developing before their second birthday.[5] "Very few Christian parents are intentionally focused on developing the worldview of their children."[6] Families are distracted away from family altars to the convenience of entertainment piped directly into their living room.[7]

CAN JESUS FIX THIS?

We see the rise and fall of nations, from godliness to moral decline, both biblically and historically throughout the ages. But Jesus, knowing the condition of man, left us a strategy—and if we will follow His simple yet profound plan, we will see the nation restored. His plan was concentric—that we would start from home and move to the nation and the nations of the earth. As Jesus pointed out: "You will be My witnesses in Jerusalem and in all Judea, and Samaria, and to the end of the earth" in the power of the Holy Spirit (see Acts 1:8). Throughout the entire book of Acts, we see the disciples taking the Good News of Jesus Christ into their homes and communities and it turned the world upside down. This same strategy will work today.

Let's take a look at how the strategy of Jesus transforms a nation.

THE STORY OF UGANDA

I spoke in Chapter 2 about the revival taking place in Uganda, a country that was experiencing severe violence, persecution, AIDS, and other social woes. When Christians in Uganda started family altars, they saw many of these issues resolved. God told them that their nation's transformation would begin in the home: "Every Christian household should be a prayer altar."

The Lord spoke to one key Ugandan leader, "I am calling for every individual Christian to start praying. Let every Christian family start praying together and let there be prayer going on in every church. Let Christians start prayer in their workplaces. By doing that, you will be giving me legal ground to work in your land."[8]

The Ugandans had not heard the term "legal ground." The Lord showed them this was not a new thing. God brought to memory the strategy He had given Abraham to take the land of Canaan, what the Ugandans refer to as the "Abrahamic Strategy." The Lord told Abraham to look north and south, east and west. *"Go, walk through the length and breadth of the land, for I am giving it to you"* (Gen. 13:17 NIV).

The Lord told the Ugandans the same thing, "Wherever you go throughout your nation, set up altars of prayer and call on the name of the Lord." This is also how God worked through the early Church to begin to occupy territory, advance His Kingdom, break the powers of darkness, and draw His presence.

My friend Chris was a youth pastor in Florida. Through his church, he became connected with the Ugandan "prayer altars" movement. Subsequently, he was asked to be its media director. For Chris, this began a journey into understanding the transformational power of prayer altars. Chris traveled to Uganda with the assignment to interview some 30-plus individuals, to hear their stories of how the revival began. He had seen videos of the revival taking place there and the large stadium events where multiple thousands were worshiping and praying together for their nation. He had even seen where, at one large stadium event, their leader, President Yoweri Museveni, had proclaimed Uganda to be a Christian nation.

Chris shared that it was only as he interviewed these individuals, and each one separately talked about the importance of the family altar, that it became clear that this was the foundation where the revival began. They shared stories of how marriages were healed, prodigals came home, and family members were delivered from addictions. The presence of God was everywhere, in every area of their lives, work, and nation.

One day, when I was talking with Chris, he shared a story of what happened while he was staying as a guest in the home of a high-ranking Ugandan government official. The man—I will call him Adroa—had a demanding schedule. He was up early every morning and came home late at night. He and his wife had eight children, ranging in age from five years old to early twenties. In spite of these obstacles, the family had an extended time of prayer every evening.

Chris recounts these as being fiery times of fervent prayer and engaging worship. One night, Chris came back to their home exhausted from jet lag and a long day of filming. He quietly slipped in the door and headed to his bedroom, hoping no one would ask him to come out. He desperately needed sleep. As Chris lay in bed, he heard the prayer altar getting started. The presence of the Lord began to permeate his room. The aroma of the worship rose higher and higher. Soon, Chris could no longer stay in his room. He jumped out of bed and said, "I have to be a part of this!"

From their homes, the Ugandan Christians expanded their prayer altars and invited the Holy Spirit into their workplaces. Many Ugandan business owners started establishing prayer altars and seeing their workers come to Christ. The business owners and managers now testify of changing their business practices. As they seek to draw His presence, some find they need to operate with more integrity, while others find they need to treat their employees better. These changes have dramatically impacted other businesses in their industry.

A TV producer was hearing testimonies from around his nation of people experiencing the presence of God as they were establishing altars of prayer in their workplaces. He heard stories about how God was changing their industries to be more ethical, blessing their businesses and workers, and how God's presence markedly impacted productivity and profit.

This man began to draw together his crew to read the Bible for 30 or 40 minutes, and then spend time praising the God they had read about in the Scriptures. As they did this, nothing happened; they did not experience or see evidence of God's tangible presence. So, this producer humbled himself and asked, "God, why are these other workplaces experiencing Your presence and we are not?"

After a time of seeking the Lord, God showed him that the TV shows they were producing were not glorifying to Him. So, the producer told the actors, scriptwriters, and others in the studio they needed to start creating materials that were more glorifying to God. The crew began again to read the Scriptures and praise the Lord together. This time people were converted, and their hearts were changed and unified with this man's Christ-honoring vision. This marketplace altar even started to have an impact in their industry.[9]

> In almost all the places of work in Uganda today, every company and corporation, you will find there is a fellowship. These fellowships were non-existent a few years ago but today almost everywhere you go you find a fellowship of people from different churches and congregations, various denominations coming together under the name of Jesus for their place of work. That is how prayer was started in the President's office, in the Bank of Uganda and other banks...prayer was started among bankers, among lawyers. The revenue authority people started an altar of prayer that totally changed the Ugandan Revenue Authority. Today it's like in every major hotel in the city, services are being conducted. Talk about Parliament, talk about the statehouse, every sector of life has been affected.[10]

When my husband, Hal, visited Kampala, Uganda, a few years ago, He was surprised to walk into a bank or supermarket and hear Christian worship music being played, and when he visited the tourist area to see shop owners sitting and openly reading their Bibles. He said, "Everywhere you went, people were talking about Jesus!"

PRAYER ALTARS IN EAST ASIA

This same transformation is happening in other nations. East Asia is experiencing change through establishing sustained prayer and worship to seek and draw the presence of God. I will tell you a story about a businessman—I will call him Nathan—who was a division head in one facet of a mobile phone manufacturing plant. He carried a considerable level of responsibility. When Nathan asked the Lord what he could do for Him at work, the Lord replied, "Just invite Me in." So, that's what Nathan did!

At the time, only 2-3 percent of the nation's population were Christians. Though Nathan's office was predominately Buddhist, he started a corporate gathering with several other Christ-followers. Together they read the Bible aloud, worshiped the Lord, and prayed for their workplace. Soon, other workers began to join them and started accepting Christ.

Just as they did at home in their family altars, these workers asked God if anything was hindering Him from moving in the plant. The Lord showed them *they* were actually a part of the problem! They were inflating the numbers on their weekly reports at their boss's request. Nathan put his job on the line; he told his boss he couldn't do that anymore.

The boss said, "Then get someone else to do that for you!"

To this, Nathan replied, "Well, I can't do that either."

Nathan didn't understand why he wasn't fired, but God spared his job. As Nathan repented for lying and supporting financial compromise, God's Spirit began to move in the office with more and more workers coming to faith in Jesus. Initially only a handful, the group grew to ten, twenty, thirty, and then 50 people gathered to worship Jesus.

As Nathan prayed, the Holy Spirit convicted him of another sin. The plant kept workers so late at night to meet their quotas that their families were suffering. There was no time for them to go home and lead their families into a lifestyle of seeking God together.

Nathan risked his job again by letting his employees go home at 6 p.m. and not forcing overtime.

Meanwhile, productivity in Nathan's department continued to increase, becoming the highest-producing department in the plant. One day, while he and the other workers were praying and reading the Bible during the lunch break, the boss came in and said: "Tell me what you are doing in here! You are the highest-producing department in the plant. I want to know what you are doing to achieve these results." Nathan explained that they were praying and honoring God, and that God was blessing their work.

"Whatever you are doing here, we want you to share this with the other department heads," the boss told Nathan. "We have scheduled a meeting for you to share with them for one hour." At the meeting, Nathan gave a five-point presentation. Slide one: "*The fear of the Lord is the beginning of wisdom*" (Prov. 9:10 NIV).[11] Last slide: Jesus is the solution to all our problems.

Churches came under the conviction of the Holy Spirit that they needed to help their congregation learn to establish a lifestyle of prayer and worship in their families. One church in Taiwan with approximately 1,500 members began to teach about personal prayer altars and how our heart is the first altar that must be built. The church began to equip and instruct the congregation on how to minister to the Lord, make the Word of God the centerpiece of their lives, and draw the presence of God so the fire in their hearts would not go out. The Lord gave them the vision to see at least 60 percent of the people in the congregation establishing family prayer and worship in their homes. The leadership prayed for this goal and established family prayer altars in their own homes. This church fought through the obstacles, challenges, and time constraints that made doing this difficult, and experienced many breakthroughs and transformed lives, marriages, and families.[12]

There were testimonies of marriages that were changed, extended family members brought to Christ out of Buddhism or ancestral worship—all because of the presence of God in their homes. They shared how neighbors were won to Christ and children began to catch fire for the Lord again.

The testimonies of the change in this church became so noticeable that other churches around them began to request their help to establish prayer altars for their families too. This was just one church's story, but there were hundreds and hundreds more churches. Within three years, altars of prayer and worship were established in all seventeen provinces of the nation. The atmosphere in churches, families, and communities began to change and become more conducive to the Gospel. The change was so evident that Christian leaders outside Taiwan, including South Korea, Hong Kong, Malaysia, and mainland China, also began to take note.[13]

THE TRANSFORMING FIRE OF REVIVAL

Together we've just looked at stories and reviewed models of transforming revival. If you want to see the same results in your nation, what principles must you take away and apply in your own life and family?

Recognize We Are in a Culture War

It's essential to understand that we and our families are not wrestling with human reason and cultural ideologies, but we are in a spiritual battle against humanistic philosophies and belief systems. Our most powerful weapon is the truth of God's Word, so if we are to win the culture war, you and I must develop the habit and discipline of thinking about all things biblically.

One of satan's most effective lies has been to divide our sense of reality into two categories, sacred and secular. Many Christians consider the sacred to be separate from the secular and thus apply the Bible's teachings solely to what they believe to be sacred. This primarily includes God, religion, church, salvation, and personal holiness. Then everything else is seen as secular—politics, business, economics, the arts, marriage, and family. We mistakenly respond to the "secular" arenas by taking our cues from the prevailing cultural trends and its accepted norms and practices, regardless of how God's Word speaks to such things. We cannot change or influence cultural norms if we do not live differently than the way those without a knowledge of Christ live (see Rom. 12:2).

It's Time to Stop Vacillating Between Two Opinions

As we've seen in the stories throughout this book, the flow of God's blessings, His presence and power are hindered when we compromise God's truth in any area of our lives. God calls us to renew our thinking and stop straddling the fence between living according to God's Word and living according to the prevailing culture. "*Choose today whom you will serve*" (Josh. 24:15 NLT). A divided heart leads to unstable actions and ultimately destruction. Remember Elijah's cry: "*How much longer will you waver, hobbling between two opinions? If the Lord is God, follow him! But if Baal is God, then follow him!*" (1 Kings 18:21 NLT). What is your response?

He Is Lord of All

God is the Lord of all—both in Heaven and earth. His truth applies to all areas of our life, public and private. We must commit to changing our mindset and acknowledge the lordship of Christ over every area of life—home, work, and play—and regarding every cultural issue. If we desire to walk in God's favor, blessings, and power, we must embrace His Word as the handbook for all of life, marriage, family, raising children, succeeding in the workplace, and solving the problems of our world.

God's Word and Presence Transform Culture

God does not have a contingency plan. Transforming revival will only come through His people. Revival does not just fall out of the sky on our heads. Just as electrical wires receive a transference of electricity when they are aligned with the power source, when we are aligned with God's Word, we attract His presence and power.

The Transformation of Our Nation Begins at Home

Revival is like a fire; it starts, moves outward, and spreads. That's why it's often called "revival fire." This is what I believe I saw in my vision: revived individuals and families, walking in God's truth and values, transforming our nation in the power of the Holy Spirit!

ACTIVATION: ESTABLISHING CORPORATE PRAYER AND WORSHIP

1. Take some time to reflect on how Christ-followers can influence culture by inviting God's presence into every area inside and outside their homes.

2. Ask the Lord to show you how to start a corporate prayer altar at your school, workplace, or other places where you serve in the community. Consider the school or workplace guidelines you would need to

adhere to. Ask the Lord to give you favor, to open doors for you, and give wisdom for the proper first steps to take.

3. Pray about who you could invite to join you in asking the Holy Spirit to change the spiritual atmosphere and to work in the hearts of the people in this place. Engage them to begin praying alongside you for God's plan and how to implement it.

4. As a family, pray with one another about your vision for prayer in your school or workplace. Ask the Lord to empower you and your family with His Holy Spirit for this assignment.

5. Ask Him to use you and your family as catalysts to bring godly change to every sphere of influence He has given you.

LET'S PRAY

Heavenly Father, You are the all-powerful God. The name of Jesus is above every other name. I ask that Your Holy Spirit would come upon me and impart ability, power, efficiency, and might. Mighty God, empower me to be a catalyst to bring change to the spiritual climate of my school, workplace, and areas of community service. Give me wisdom, favor, and clarity in this assignment. I decree that Your holy presence is abiding and pushing back the darkness in the places where I study, work, and serve. In Jesus' name. Amen.

CHAPTER 12

ATTRACTING THE FIRE: WHAT INVITES GOD'S PRESENCE?

And he [Elijah] repaired the altar of the Lord that was broken down...then the fire of the Lord fell (1 Kings 18:30,38 KJV).

"Return to me, and I will return to you," says the Lord Almighty (Malachi 3:7 NIV).

When I was four years old my family moved next door to the Johnsons. Their daughter, Alida, who was my same age, became my best friend. In those days we didn't lock our doors. So, whenever I wanted to visit Alida, I'd just walk across the driveway that separated our homes, open the back door, and walk into their house, anytime day or night. As I'd walk past the living room, I would often see my friend's mother kneeling in prayer in front of a chair or beside the sofa. This left a deep, lasting impression on my young heart. When I think back, what I remember most about their house was that it felt like God lived there.

At those moments I could feel the presence of an unseen Person who I intuitively sensed wanted me to draw near to Him. These were my first encounters with a prayer altar. I will never forget the sense of reverence and awe I felt. Prayer altars are contagious because the Holy Spirit is present in those times and places. You never know how powerfully your own personal altar will influence the people in your household and even others in the households around you.

Throughout history, rebuilding the altar of the Lord has always signified the return of God's people to Him. Our Lord is looking for hearts that are completely His. Scripture tells us that if we seek Him with all of our heart, we will find Him (see Jer. 29:13). In fact, it is impossible to pursue God and not encounter Him. If we draw near to God, He promises that He will draw near to us (see James 4:8).

The Lord is jealous for our attention, companionship, and relationship. He says to us, "*You must worship no other gods, for the Lord, whose very name is Jealous, is a God who is jealous about his relationship with you*" (Exod. 34:14 NLT). He declares, "*you shall be my people, and I will be your God*" (Jer. 30:22 ESV). The altar has always been the place where the Lord and His people meet to establish and affirm our covenant with Him. In a biblical sense, a "covenant" is a commitment between two parties, making them one. God promised His chosen people to be their Father, friend, provider, and protector. In return, His "chosen" would offer their loving devotion, respect, and submission; we would stay close and follow Him. Like in a marriage, the bride and groom exchange vows to love, honor, and cherish one another for life; this is the same promise the Lord gave to His chosen bride, us!

Throughout the ages God's people have vacillated between worshiping God and straying away from Him to follow after worldly pursuits. All throughout the Bible when God's people turned away from Him—began to run after other gods—the first thing we notice is that their altars (places of worship) were neglected and fell into disrepair. The people forgot they were in covenant with the Lord, that they belonged to Him.

We see in Scripture that when God's people (Israel) realized they were on the wrong path, that they had forsaken their God, the first thing they did was tear down their unholy altars and then rebuild the altar of the Lord—the place of relationship with Him. This happened over and over again.

The cycle went something like this: God's people worshiped the one true and living God, and He blessed, prospered, and protected them. In their peace and prosperity, they forgot the Lord, and their hearts were drawn away to worship other gods (people, activities, pursuits). They soon lost the blessings and favor of God, were overtaken by their enemies, and fell into bondage. Then they woke up and realized they were no longer under the protection and blessings of the Lord—that they had sinned and fallen away from Him. When they repented and cried out to the Lord, He graciously forgave them and delivered them from their captivity. When God's beloved people began to worship Him once more, He blessed, prospered, and protected them. But it was not long before they got caught up in their peace and prosperity and grew complacent. Their hearts were once again drawn away. And so, the cycle repeated itself (see the book of Judges).

THE GREATEST ALTAR: THE CROSS OF CALVARY

Restoring the altar of the Lord for fresh fire today is not about build-ing a physical altar or maintaining a natural fire. The altar God desires today is a heart fully committed to Him. For you and me, as God's people, restoring the altar of our hearts to maintain the spiritual fire of God's presence is our highest aim. Remember, the Old Testament altar was simply a foreshadowing of what was to come through our relationship with Jesus Christ. In fact, the most important altar of sacrifice ever built—the one that forever altered history—was the cross of Calvary. The cross was the altar built of wood, and Jesus was the Lamb of God, the perfect sacrifice, offered for the forgiveness of our sins and the sins of the world.

When I was a child during my elementary and junior high school years, my family and I attended a Bible-believing denomi-national church. I enjoyed going to the special classes on Sunday and Wednesday nights where I studied the Bible and memorized Scrip-ture. I loved church, and I felt a close relationship with the Lord. One night our teacher shared the story of Lottie Moon, a mission-ary to China. The teacher talked about how God calls some people to serve Him in vocational ministry. She quoted from Isaiah 6:8 (NIV): *"Whom shall I send? And who will go for us?"* And just as Isaiah answered, I said, "Here am I, Lord, send me!"

During my high school years, my family rarely went to church. I fell in with a new group of friends, almost none of whom were Christians. When I went away to college, I'm not sure I even took my Bible with me. I seldom attended church, and though I didn't totally walk away from the Lord, my relationship with Him was distant, and I was strongly influenced by college and sorority life.

By my senior year, I was feeling empty, unfulfilled, searching— as if I'd somehow lost my way. The Holy Spirit began to speak to me that I was on the wrong path. He began to give me a hunger and desire to come back to a deep relationship with the Lord. I wasn't close to any deeply committed Christians on campus. But one day I walked over to the Baptist Student Union. As I entered, I realized I was the only one there. I looked around and noticed a small kneeling altar in one area of the room. There I knelt and rededicated my life to Christ. Rebuilding the altar is always the place of returning to the Lord. When we begin to neglect our times of worship and prayer with Him, it is the first indication that our relationship with Jesus Christ is in danger of growing cold and distant. Restoring the altar is significant because it demonstrates that we have come home to Him.

THE BATTLE OF TWO ALTARS

And Elijah said unto all the people, Come near unto me. And all the people came near unto him. And he repaired the altar of the Lord that was broken down (1 Kings 18:30 KJV).

I won't take the time to retell in its entirety this familiar Bible story. I will, however, briefly fill you in on the background of what is happening in the events surrounding this passage of Scripture. I believe the Lord is speaking loudly to us through this passage. Let's revisit this story and draw some important conclusions for our lives, families, and nations today.

When Ahab rose to power in Israel, along with his wicked wife, Jezebel, he led the nation of Israel into worshiping false gods. He even set out to murder all of the prophets of the one true God. The prophet Elijah became a real thorn in Ahab's side. God protected Elijah against Ahab's murderous threats—no matter how hard Ahab tried, he could not lay a hand on him. The events of 1 Kings 18:30 take place as the dramatic conflict between them comes to its climax.

At God's instruction, Elijah came out of hiding. He sent word to Ahab that he was ready for the showdown between the God of Israel and the false god of Ahab's priests, Baal. Baal was among the most prominent idols mentioned in the Bible. He was the god of the weather, rain, and harvest. The land of Israel was in a severe drought, so the misguided people of Israel began to worship this false god of the weather, hoping for rain and a good harvest. Ahab sent all his priests of Baal to meet Elijah for a showdown on Mount Carmel. This would become a great supernatural confrontation with the God of Elijah against Ahab's Baal. The prophets of Baal went first. They prepared their bull as a sacrifice and placed it on an altar for Baal. Then they prayed to Baal, asking him to send fire down to the altar. They prayed all morning; they prayed nonstop until noon, but nothing happened. The priests even danced around their altar. But Baal didn't answer.

At noon, Elijah began to taunt them. "Shout louder!" he said. "I'm sure Baal is a god! Maybe he is busy right now. Or perhaps he's away on a trip. Maybe he's sleeping. Shout a little louder; you might need to wake him up." The prophets of Baal shouted louder and louder. They continued praying and shouting with all their might until evening. But there was no response.

When they finally gave up, Elijah gathered the people to himself. "Come," he said, "and help me repair the altar of the Lord that is broken down." The nation of Israel had fallen out of relationship with their God and turned to idolatry; they were experiencing God's judgment. This great prophet of God, Elijah, was about to demonstrate the power of God and call them back from the verge of total destruction to a place of repentance and restoration. To this end, Elijah first pointed out that the altar of the Lord was broken down and needed repair.

There was a significant link between the condition of God's altar and the broken state of the nation. When the nation neglected its relationship with the God of Israel, it would spiral into decline. There would be a free fall into hypocrisy and moral and spiritual decay until they reached a place of absolute apostasy. The priests of God, His chosen and elect, would all drift into the clutches of idolatry whenever they abandoned their worship of God.

The altar of God was the best barometer of the spiritual condition of the nation of Israel. It was the place God had chosen to meet with His covenant people. Whenever the altar is abandoned or neglected, whenever communion with the Lord no longer matters, that is the time sin gains a stronghold in the hearts of the people and starts to reign in the midst of the nation. The writer of Proverbs says that *"righteousness exalts a nation, but sin is a reproach to any people"* (Prov. 14:34 ESV). In other words, when the people of a nation are in a right relationship with God, He exalts and prospers the people of that land. The same is true of a family or an individual.

Scripture confirms this time and time again. I cannot overemphasize how important it is to have a right relationship with God. It's akin to lighting and tending the altar (staying in worship and fellowship with the Lord).

The Israelites' altar was never to be abandoned or God's fire abandoned. It was to be an active part of their everyday lives. The altar was a place for people to be regularly reminded that their greatest calling in life was to worship and serve the Lord. It was at the altar that the sacrifice and the fire constantly spoke to the nation of Israel that they didn't become great by their own power. They didn't get there by their own works. They didn't owe their victories to their armies' strength or the warriors' skill. Their greatness wasn't in their natural resources or the wealth they may have amassed.

The fire on the altar reminded them that the thing that made them great was the presence of a Holy God in their midst! It was God and their worship and service to Him that had exalted them above other nations. It was God who had set them apart, God who had provided for them, God who had made a way when there was no way. The altar served as a constant reminder not to rely on themselves, not to depend on their own strength, but to remember that the presence of God was their greatest asset. When they neglected the altar, they neglected God!

This is as true for us today as it was for the Israelites. The altar was then and is now a place to meet with God and worship Him. The altar remains the place we enjoy our personal connection with God. The declaration you are making by dedicating your altar—establishing a regular time to meet with Him—will challenge you to put Him first. It will compel you to put His Kingdom, and His will for your life, above everything else. This is the time and place you build relationship with God—and where the things that hinder your walk with Him are consumed in the fires of His presence.

A PLATFORM FOR THE FIRE TO FALL

The condition of our altars is the best indicator of whether our relationship with the Lord is hot or cold. The altars of Israel were broken down and no one seemed to care or even notice. So, Elijah gathered the people and rebuilt the Lord's altar that had been neglected. He rebuilt it with twelve large stones, placing firewood in proper order on top of the stones and digging a ditch around the altar. He prepared the bull as a sacrifice and placed it on top of the wood.

Then Elijah did something astounding: he told the people to fill four barrels with water and pour them out on the altar over and over again. They soaked the sacrifice and the wood, and filled the trenches with water, drenching the altar. Since the challenge was for God to answer by fire, Elijah made sure that when the fire fell, everyone would know that only God could have done it.

Finally, when it was time to offer the evening sacrifice, Elijah stepped forward. He prayed: *"Hear me, O Lord, hear me, that this people may know that You are the Lord God, and that You have turned their hearts back to You again"* (1 Kings 18:37 NKJV). And when he prayed, the fire of the Lord fell from Heaven and consumed the burnt sacrifice, the wood, the stones, and the dust, even licking up the water that was in the trench.

This is what happens when you build your altar God's way—you create a platform in your life and family for God to show Himself powerfully. When Elijah rebuilt the Israelites' altar, he set the stage for the mighty miraculous outpouring of the presence of God.

ATTRACTING THE FIRE OF GOD!

Remember, Elijah rebuilt the altar with twelve large stones. These represented the twelve tribes of Israel, the twelve families who were Jacob's sons. We might draw the analogy that our family members are the stones of our altar—whether our family is made up of one person or many more. We come together to form the altar of worship and create an atmosphere that attracts God's Holy Spirit.

The wood provided the fuel for the fire. Wood represents our strength, giftings, and life's work. Everything God has given us we offer back to Him. The Bible reminds us that a day will come when everything we have accomplished in life will be tested by fire. Whatever is impure, done out of wrong motives or in our own strength will be burned up, purified, and refined. The Bible calls this "wood, hay, and stubble" (see 1 Cor. 3:12-15). These temporary things can seem important and desirable in the moment but, ultimately, don't last. These are the very things God wants us and our families to surrender as fuel for the fire on the altar every time we come to Him.

And what about the sacrifice? Our sacrifices are our best gifts offered to God—consecrated (set apart) for His special purpose. As believers, we offer our very selves to God. In Romans 12:1 (NIV), Paul says, "*I urge you, brothers and sisters, in view of God's mercy, to offer your bodies as a living sacrifice, holy and pleasing to God—this is your true and proper worship.*" Because Jesus, the Holy Lamb of God, gave Himself for us, it's reasonable and proper for us to present ourselves as a living sacrifice every time we come to the altar. The altar then is a place of total surrender. We offer to the Lord all that we are and all that we do. We surrender *all* to Him.

Often, we see people kneeling in prayer. This demonstrates their act of surrender—just as I saw my friend's mother doing in her living room, as I did in the Baptist Student Union when I was in college, as people still do in some churches today. It's what Jesus did in the Garden of Gethsemane as He prepared Himself for His ultimate sacrifice on the cross. This action of the heart is first and foremost what attracts the fire of God—our complete and wholehearted giving of ourselves and family to Him.

ACTIVATION: PUTTING EVERYTHING ON THE ALTAR

1. Spend some time with the Lord and reflect on the answers to these questions:

   - What do I need to surrender to the Lord? What areas of my life do I need to give to Him?

   - What problems or situations in my family need to be laid on the altar?

2. The next time you gather your family to pray, ask your family members: "What do you personally need to surrender to the Lord? What do you feel we, as a family, need to surrender to the Lord? What are the mountains that only He can move? Are there any problems we have been trying to fix ourselves?"

3. Then together, in prayer, lay these issues on the altar—give them to Him—and ask Him for a mighty outpouring of His Spirit to empower You to do what He is asking of you and to accomplish what only He can do!

LET'S PRAY

Dear Lord, I come before You just as I am and dedicate my whole life to You. I give my family afresh and anew to You—every family member, every problem, every impossible situation. I lay it all on the altar. Forgive me for trying to fix the problems in my life and family in my own wisdom and strength. I know You have said that we cannot move mountains in our own might or by our own power, but it is by Your Spirit. Come Holy Spirit and empower us to restore any broken or distant places in our relationship with the Father and with one another. We decree that as a family we are going to follow the Lord more closely and to honor Him daily in all we do. Amen.

CHAPTER 13

WHEN THE FIRE FALLS:
KEEP THE FLAME BURNING!

I indeed baptize you with water unto repentance, but He who is coming after me is mightier than I, whose sandals I am not worthy to carry. He will baptize you with the Holy Spirit and fire (Matthew 3:11 NKJV).

You may have already established your family altar. You've set aside times to gather your family to pray and worship the Lord in your home. Or you have assembled all the knowledge needed to create a plan to get started. Now it's time to call for the fire of God to come, just as the prophet Elijah did!

What is the fire of God? Why was it so vital that the Lord's command to the priests was to keep the fire on the altar burning—so that it would never go out? And what does that mean for our lives and homes today?

WHAT IS THE "FIRE OF GOD"?

The Bible describes God Himself as fire: *"a consuming fire"* (Heb. 12:29 ESV). Fire communicates, first of all, the very presence of God. The authors of the Bible also portrayed fire as God's power, holiness, light, and protection over His people. These are the very attributes that we want to burn brightly in our lives and homes.

It is not always possible to distinguish the presence of God from His glory, for His glory radiates His beauty, character, and power—which we can experience as His "presence."

Scripture often portrays God's glory as "fire." An excellent example of this is when the children of Israel encountered the fire of God's glory at Mount Sinai, where Moses went up to meet with God to receive the Ten Commandments. To the Israelites, the glory of the Lord looked like a consuming fire on top of the mountain (see Exod. 24:17; Lev. 9:23-24; Deut. 5:24), and they experienced His "presence" as an overpowering manifestation of His beauty, character, and power. They felt this so strongly that they couldn't bear it and asked for Moses to speak with them instead of God Himself.

Later in Israel's history, King Solomon built and dedicated God's Temple, and:

> *As soon as Solomon finished his prayer, fire came down from heaven and consumed the burnt offering and the sacrifices [on the altar], and the glory of the Lord filled the temple. And the priests could not enter the house of the Lord, because the glory of the Lord filled the Lord's house. When all the people of Israel saw the fire come down and the glory of the Lord on the temple, they bowed down with their faces to the ground on the*

pavement and worshiped and gave thanks to the Lord, saying, "For he is good, for his steadfast love endures forever" (2 Chronicles 7:1-3 ESV).

This is a powerful story! As these verses illustrate, the glory of the Lord fills the temple when the fire falls. The Lord desires to do this in your heart and home as you meet with Him at the family altar—He wants to fill you with the fire of His glorious presence!

My good friend Stephanie shares how she and her husband, Steve, fiercely contended at their family altar for God's fire to fall and heal their son of a devastating disease.

At one and a half years of age our son, Steve, Jr.—we call him "Stevie"—was diagnosed with juvenile rheumatoid arthritis (JRA). Statistically, 80 percent of children grow out of this condition within six months. For Stevie, the condition only got worse. He was taking eight tablespoons of Motrin a day to help with inflammation and pain. This went on until he was seven years old.

One day my mom called to share that there was going to be a healing service at her church that Sunday night. She suggested we bring Stevie to be prayed for.

In the church service, Stevie would not be quiet or sit still. Out of my spirit flowed the words to the song, "Nothing but the Blood of Jesus." I sang these words over my son again and again all throughout the church service.

When it was Stevie's turn to be prayed for, the presence of God was so strong I could barely stand. The minister told me: "Now I want you to start walking your son back and forth, up and down the aisle." A few minutes after we started doing this, Stevie said his leg started to feel like it was burning. He began screaming: "My knee is on fire! My knee is on fire!"

That night God healed my son. His heavenly fire burned up the JRA disease! It has been 20 years now and Stevie has no signs or symptoms of JRA. Our family knows what it's like to sacrifice in prayer upon the altar and experience God's fire.

FIRE AND THE FEAR OF THE LORD

The most prevalent word for *fire* in Hebrew is אֵשׁ, pronounced "*es*," and its paleo-root meaning is the "great destroyer." When we look at the individual Hebrew letters that spell out *fire* in the "fire of God," we discover that the *aleph* (א), the first letter in the Hebrew alphabet, represents an ox—strength or power—and the Hebrew letter *shen* (שׁ) represents teeth, meaning to destroy or consume.

Because of their meanings, the combination of these two letters makes up the Hebrew word for *fire,* which translates to "the strong destroyer." The "fire of God" literally means "God is a consuming fire."

From our earliest age, we learn to respect fire's power, potential, and danger. Fire will destroy; it will burn until nothing is left but ash. However, we also appreciate fire's benefits: if handled wisely, fire will provide warmth, prepare our food, and provide light and fuel. So it is with God's glory.

As you and I assess our lives, we ought to be mindful that we might have a relationship with God (appreciating His benefits), yet at the same time neglect to fear Him and respect His power—failing to give Him the awe, respect, and reverence He deserves!

A lack of the "fear of the Lord" is like having a relationship with someone important from whom you will not receive their counsel, obey their warnings, or show honor or respect. To have an intimate and meaningful relationship with God, the Creator of Heaven and earth, you must humbly respect and take Him seriously, just as you would handle coals of fire.

Fear of God is not being afraid of Him; it is to live set apart from the world's influences in holy respect, reverence, and awe of God. The fear of God and His Word keeps us from a broken relationship with Him. You take His Word seriously and without compromise. This happens when you embrace and respect His Word in your heart and in your home.

In response, the Lord draws close; you can feel His presence. Every time you go to the family altar, there is a sense of awe and respect—that you are coming into the presence of Almighty God. When you come before the Lord in this way, you can expect to come away from your time with Him and step out into the world with the fire of God's presence shining on your face and through your life.

HOW IS THE HOLY SPIRIT LIKE A FIRE?

At the very beginning of the New Testament, the Holy Spirit is associated with fire. John the Baptist declared: "*I indeed baptize you with water unto repentance, but He who is coming after me is mightier than I, whose sandals I am not worthy to carry.* **He will baptize you with the Holy Spirit and fire**" (Matt. 3:11 NKJV).

When the Holy Spirit began His ministry of indwelling the early Church, He chose to appear as "tongues of fire" resting on the believers who had assembled in the upper room:

> *When the day of Pentecost arrived, they were all together in one place. And suddenly there came from heaven a sound like a mighty rushing wind, and it filled the entire house where they were sitting. And divided tongues as of fire appeared to them and rested on each one of them* (Acts 2:1-3 ESV).

Through this passage, we see that fiery tongues were a manifestation of the third Person of the Godhead, the Holy Spirit, a theological concept unseen in the Old Testament.

I want to ask you an important question: "Is the fire of the Holy Spirit burning brightly upon the altar of your heart?"

This is essentially the same question the apostle Paul asked some disciples he met walking down the road as he passed through Ephesus: *"Did you receive the Holy Spirit when you believed?"* (Acts 19:2 ESV).

They told him, *"No, we have not even heard that there is a Holy Spirit."* Paul then proceeded to lay hands on them and, as he did, the Holy Spirit came upon them (see Acts 19:6). Jesus spoke of His gift of the Holy Spirit, given freely to those who ask:

> *Which of you fathers, if your son asks for a fish, will give him a snake instead? Or if he asks for an egg, will give him a scorpion? If you then, though you are evil, know how to give good gifts to your children, how much more*

will your Father in heaven give the Holy Spirit to those who ask him! (Luke 11:11-13 NIV)

In other words, if your son asks for his essential needs, such as food to give him strength, you will not deny him. In the same way, if you ask the Lord for the gift of the Holy Spirit to give you strength and power to serve Him, how much more will He do that for you?

As a believer in Jesus Christ who has accepted His sacrifice on the cross for your sins and surrendered your life to Him, you can ask and receive the gift of the Holy Spirit and fire.

- Is the altar ready?
- Is the wood in place?
- Are you surrendered as a living sacrifice?
- Ask for the fire to fall!

Jesus says, "*Until now you have asked nothing in my name. Ask, and you will receive, that your joy may be full*" (John 16:24 ESV). When you ask, you will surely not be disappointed!

KEEP THE FLAME BURNING

The Lord's command to the priests was that the fire kindled from the throne of Heaven was never to go out: "*Fire shall be kept burning on the altar continually; it shall not go out*" (Lev. 6:13 ESV). The reason the ongoing fire was so important is that it was lit originally by God Himself: "*Fire came out from the presence of the Lord and consumed the burnt offering and the fat portions on the altar. And when all the people saw it, they shouted for joy and fell facedown*" (Lev.

9:24 NIV). The fire on the altar, therefore, represented God's power and presence continually with His people. It was a gift from Heaven.

The Holy Spirit's fire is still God's gift to us today. This fire, God's fire, is a living fire! His desire is that you burn with His presence perpetually!

Our role is to keep the fire burning, just as the priests did, because *"you are royal priests, a holy nation, God's very own possession"* (1 Pet. 2:9 NLT). In your passionate desire for life-changing encounters with God, you must not let your fire go out as you cry out for His presence and power in your life and home. True worship and communion with the Lord must become a lifestyle.

Know that you will need to fiercely guard and tend to your altar, contending for its priority in your life and family (see John 10:10). The enemy will try to push back against you and distract you from your relationship with God. The devil will fight for your attention, not conceding territory readily. He may come at you like a roaring lion, but God has empowered you by His Word and Spirit to overcome him (see 1 Pet. 5:8-9; James 4:7). God keeps His promise and will not allow you to be tested beyond your power to remain firm. The Lord is faithful; He will strengthen you and guard you from the evil one (see 2 Thess. 3:3).

Challenges will come against you to shorten or disrupt your time at the family altar; the enemy will attempt to discourage you, sidetrack your prayers and worship, or convince you that it's not making a difference. You may find your mind wandering while pressing into the Lord. You may, on occasion, find yourself setting aside your time for other things or losing interest.

We all experience this kind of struggle. When this happens, share your heart honestly with the Lord. Cry out to Him and ask Him to draw you back to Himself. If you make the first move toward the Lord, He will move toward you (see James 4:8). If you fell into something that broke your relationship with someone in your family, be willing to go and ask for forgiveness and reconcile that relationship with the Lord's help. You must keep your heart's altar pure and your life and family a priority.

When you discern that the enemy is strategically trying to shut down your intimacy with God, press in deeper to the Lord. Learn how to step up *more* boldly in Christ's authority. Here are some ways to strengthen yourself in the Lord, as David did (1 Sam. 30:6):

- Make this daily commitment to yourself and the Lord: "My heart will be an altar to the Lord, and His fire will burn on it, day and night, and will not go out."

- Change your routine, so you can spend more time focusing on the Lord. Do something fresh to help you and your loved ones stay connected with God at the family altar.

- Choose to worship even if you do not feel like it. Faith will begin to rise again in your heart.

- Go for a walk or a drive in your car, or just get into a quiet place and begin to praise the Lord, turning your eyes and your attention to Him. Your praise will push away the darkness trying to come in (see Ps. 22:3 KJV).

- Put on Christian worship music or consider listening to God's Word on digital media rather than watching the news for a few days.

- Be watchful not to go on "autopilot"—where you are just going through the motions of religious activity but not noticing that something is inhibiting the work and presence of the Holy Spirit. This can happen in your personal prayer time and at your family altar.

- Be attentive and watchful to the spiritual climate in your home. After all, you are called to be a "watchman" guarding your home and family (see Ezek. 33:7; Mark 14:38).

- Read an inspiring book or devotional. Review prophetic words or Scriptures that God has given you or your family.

- Open your prayer journal (or start one if you haven't already). Remind yourself of answered prayers and all that God has done for you.

- Call a friend or prayer partner to pray and join together in agreement for your breakthrough.

LIFE IN THE HOLY SPIRIT'S PRESENCE AND POWER

Keep alert that problems and battles will attempt to storm into your life, but don't let that overcome you. Use the spiritual weapons at your disposal—such as repentance, worship, fasting with prayer, declaring Scripture, using Christ's authority to rebuke the enemy—and obtain your victory (see Luke 10:19; Acts 16:18). These weapons we use in our fight are not the world's weapons but God's mighty weapons (see 2 Cor. 10:3-5). We use them to destroy every attack of the evil one and remove the barriers and obstacles he would try to erect to prevent us from living in the presence and power of God—an "open heaven."

The reality is that the ongoing presence of the Lord in your heart and home creates a continuous "open heaven." It is like walking within a pillar of fire that acts as your protection against the spiritual powers of darkness that are at work. As you and your family develop a lifestyle of prayer, allowing your hearts to become the burning altar of God, no matter where you are or what you're doing, you will always be surrounded by God's presence. You will know how to maintain the fire of that relationship so that the heavens are continually open around you and the presence and power of the Holy Spirit remain evident in you.

As you—and more and more people in your community and nation—move in this pillar of fire from His altar, you will carry the illuminating presence of God with you. This is how we begin to carry the spirit of revival everywhere. That's right—someone who actually walks in the presence of God brings revival!

Revival Fire Falls

As you continue to tend to the altar of the Lord, His burning presence will grow brighter and brighter in your life. History testifies of the Holy Spirit responding with fire from Heaven when believers are united in their fear of God and in passionate pursuit of His glory.

This is what happened in Scotland during the Hebrides Revival of 1949–1953. Those who lived through this move of God testified that the distinguishing characteristic of the revival was the awesome fear of God that gripped the souls of men and women. Witnesses related that a profound feeling of emptiness and a deep conviction of their separation from God fell upon people everywhere on the island—in their homes, at work, in the streets, the fields, churches, and even at the police station.

The Hebrides Revival started in the small cottage of two sisters named Peggy and Christine Smith. At 84 and 82 years old, Peggy was completely blind and Christine was bent over with arthritis. Unable to attend church services because of their disabilities, the two gave themselves to intercessory prayer for revival to come to their village.

At that time, churches in the region were spiritually dead. Legalism was extreme. Not one young person was in church. Yet Peggy and Christine sensed the Lord speaking to them: *"I will pour water on the thirsty land, and streams on the dry ground; I will pour my Spirit upon your offspring, and my blessing on your descendants"* (Isa. 44:3 ESV).

Peggy and Christine spent hours in prayer, sometimes praying from 10:00 p.m. to 3:00 or 4:00 a.m. As the intercession intensified, ministers and others prayed alongside the sisters from other locations on the island, many of them in small cottages like Peggy and Christine's. People all over the island had the sense that God was telling them to "Ask Me for revival." This was divinely orchestrated!

One night, during a prayer meeting in a barn, a young man read aloud Psalm 24:3-5 (KJV):

> *Who shall ascend into the hill of the Lord? Or who shall stand in his holy place? He that hath clean hands, and a pure heart; who hath not lifted up his soul unto vanity, nor sworn deceitfully. He shall receive the blessing from the Lord, and righteousness from the God of his salvation.*

When he closed his Bible, he told those present that it seemed senseless to be praying and waiting on God if they themselves were not right with Him.

Then he prayed, "God, are *my* hands clean? Is *my* heart pure?"

Immediately, around 3:00 a.m., the presence of God gripped every person present. The groups of intercessors left the barn in the early morning hours to head home and found along the road men and women kneeling, crying out for mercy. Every home had lights on in it, as no one could sleep. The awareness of God was overwhelming!

Churches began to fill up as people returned to God. As parishioners approached the church buildings, witnesses later reported, they would fall silent in awe of the Lord. Not long after being seated inside, they would begin weeping, some from an overwhelming love of God, others due to conviction. People in the aisles and pews were on their knees, crying out for God to have mercy.

No one wanted to go home when the services were over; they would either linger at church or go into nearby homes for further instruction, fellowship, and singing. It was common for these home services to go into the late night and early morning hours. People were miraculously able to function with little to no sleep. Some would get home at 5:00 a.m., go off to work at 7:00 a.m., and work all day without getting tired!

Early one morning, 300 people, drawn by the Spirit of God, showed up at the local police station crying out to God for mercy due to overwhelming conviction of their sins. Though some attempted to run from that conviction power, it followed them wherever they went. Crime on the island became nearly non-existent.

The Hebrides Revival, which also became known as "The Cottage Revival," lasted four years, and 90 percent of the island was saved in its wake. It was a young person phenomenon. Many teenagers and those under the age of 40 were converted. The Lord was true to the word He gave the two sisters, Peggy and Christine: *"I will pour water on the thirsty land, and streams on the dry ground; I will pour my Spirit upon your offspring, and my blessing on your descendants"* (Isa. 44:3 ESV).

"IF YOU BUILD IT, I WILL COME"

Can you and I expect to see this kind of revival in our day? May it be so!

In the Upper Room, the disciples did not know what the coming move of the Holy Spirit would look like, but they prepared their altar of prayer to the Lord, and fire came from Heaven. The disciples stayed there until they were clothed with power from on high. Waiting for His presence to manifest, they knew the importance of that time; they took it very seriously and waited patiently.

When the Holy Spirit fell upon them, the disciples became altars of living stones, inviting God's Holy Spirit and fire to come and consume them as living sacrifices:

> *As you come to him, a living stone rejected by men but in the sight of God chosen and precious, you yourselves like living stones are being built up as a spiritual house, to be a holy priesthood, to offer spiritual sacrifices acceptable to God through Jesus Christ* (1 Peter 2:4-5 ESV).

You are living stones that God is building into His "spiritual house." You are a living and holy sacrifice—the kind He will find acceptable (see Rom. 12:1). This is truly the way to worship Him and wholly present yourself to God through Christ Jesus.

So great was the disciples' need for Christ's Spirit that they did not leave Jerusalem until they had all that God had promised. Their newly endowed power came from their intimate encounter with God.

We and our families are His disciples today, and we need His power just as much as they did. He is asking us to remain in the place of prayer, surrender, and worship until we encounter Him and His fire falls upon our lives and homes.

My fervent prayer is that God's Holy Spirit will empower you and your family afresh and anew, and that His holy fire will fall upon your heart, your home, and your nation.

If you will build an altar to Him, He promises to come!

APPENDIX

PRAYER GUIDES AND ACTIVATION TOOLS

A 10-DAY FAMILY PRAYER GUIDE

Day 1—Praying for Each Person's Destiny

Day 2—Praying Scripture

Day 3—Discovering Your Spiritual Gifts

Day 4—What Is Your Story?

Day 5—Decision Making

Day 6—Praying for Your Children's Schools

Day 7—Praying for Your Family's Finances

Day 8—Your Family's Future and Calling

Day 9—Cleansing Your Home from Evil Influences

Day 10—Celebrating Communion as a Family

CREATIVE IDEAS FOR FAMILY PRAYER

A Sample Family Altar

Writing a Family Covenant

Praying for Your Neighborhood

A 10-Day Family Prayer Guide

As I have talked with families of all ages and stages, many have shared with me their biggest prayer challenges, including knowing what a vibrant family prayer altar looks like, getting everyone in the family involved, and keeping them interested and engaged. With that in mind, this prayer guide provides ten creative ideas to help you develop a vital family prayer life.

You can use this guide for ten days in a row, or you can use it as a list of ideas to draw from on an intermittent basis. As you do, you can expect to see the spiritual climate of your household change.

Together, we can make an eternal difference in the lives of our families and the generations to come, as well as neighbors, friends and coworkers. The possibilities are endless when families pray!

DAY 1

PRAYING FOR EACH PERSON'S DESTINY

"For I know what I have planned for you," says the Lord, "I have plans to prosper you, not to harm you. I have plans to give you a future filled with hope" (Jeremiah 29:11 NET).

In their book *The Blessing*, Gary Smalley and John Trent write, "Children are filled with the potential to be all God intended them to be."[1] Do you realize how God has uniquely designed each member of your family?

Instructions: Ask each family member these questions:

1. What do you most often dream or daydream about?

2. When you think about being an adult (for children/ teens), what do you think you would enjoy doing?

3. Which person from the Bible would you most desire to be like? Why?

4. What is one thing you believe God may want you to do for the world?

Pray that each family member would fulfill God's unique design for their life. As you pray, if a word of encouragement comes to mind, write it in your prayer journal and share it with that family member.

Model Prayer

> Lord, we thank You that You have created (insert name) _____ as a unique individual and for a very special purpose. We ask that You would prepare _____ for the future You have planned. We pray that _____ would fulfill their God-given purpose and that every day _____ will be sensitive to Your calling and make a difference in this world!

DAY 2

PRAYING SCRIPTURE

The word of God is living and active, sharper than any double-edged sword (Hebrews 4:12 ISV).

God has given us the words in the Bible, not only to read, but to use as prayers. The more you let God's Word guide your prayers, the more you can be confident that you are praying God's will. Because the Word of God is *"full of the Spirit and life"* (John 6:63 NIV), the Holy Spirit can help you identify passages that relate to your life and family situations.

Instructions

Ask family members to find a Scripture they would like to use to craft a prayer for themselves or for someone in the family. Then take turns praying those Scriptures. You may also want to look at the requests in your prayer journal and find a Scripture promise you can pray back to God for each one.

Model Prayer

Lord, thank You for Your Word, which is alive and active and sharper than a two-edged sword. It is our delight to speak and pray Your Word, for it is full of promise. As we pray Your Word we are confident that You hear us because we are praying in agreement with Your perfect will. Thank You for giving us Your written Word, the Bible, so that we can live and pray victoriously. For You have promised, *"I will hasten my word to perform it"* (Jer. 1:12 KJV).

Day 3

Discovering Your
Spiritual Gifts

A spiritual gift is given to each of us so we can help each other. ...It is the one and only Spirit who distributes all these gifts. He alone decides which gift each person should have (1 Corinthians 12:7,11 NLT).

God has equipped His followers with various spiritual gifts. These are commonly divided into three categories:

Motivational gifts: prophesying, serving, teaching, encouraging, giving, administration, and mercy (see Rom. 12:3-8). These gifts shape how believers see their role in the Body of Christ and how they relate to and impact others.

Ministry gifts: apostles, prophets, evangelists, pastors, and teachers (see Eph. 4:11-13). These gifts build up the Church and advance God's Kingdom. They are often confirmed by ordination.

Manifestation gifts: a word of wisdom, a word of knowledge, faith, healing, working of miracles, prophecy, discerning of spirits, different kinds of tongues, and interpretation of tongues (see 1 Cor. 12:7-11). Manifestation gifts are supernatural demonstrations of the Holy Spirit's presence and power. They are manifested for the benefit of others and to bring God glory.

Instructions

As a family, ask God to reveal each person's spiritual giftings. How does He want to use each member of your family? What comes naturally to each one? Is one member gifted and passionate about organization and administration? Is another inspired to explain the things of the Lord to other people? Does a member enjoy sitting in silence, meditating on God's Word, and listening for His voice so they can share His words with others?

Ask God to show each family member how He has uniquely designed them and given them skills to encourage and build up the Church and those around them.

Model Prayer

Thank You, Lord, for designing each of us uniquely for Your purpose. Thank You for the spiritual gifts You give us by Your Spirit to encourage one another and to build Your Church. Help us to see and know our gifts and to use them wisely for advancing Your Kingdom. Amen.

DAY 4

WHAT IS YOUR STORY?

We will not hide these truths from our children; we will tell the next generation about the glorious deeds of the Lord, about his power and his mighty wonders...so the next generation might know them—even the children not yet born—and they in turn will teach their own children. So each generation should set its hope anew on God, not forgetting his glorious miracles and obeying his commands (Psalm 78:4,6-7 NLT).

Sharing stories of miracles and answers to prayer creates an atmosphere of faith, encouragement, and hope. These stories also keep our focus on the goodness and greatness of God and plant seeds of faith and expectation that will bear fruit in years to come— even for young children who hear them. This is part of God's plan for passing on the torch of faith from one generation to the next.

Instructions

When telling a miracle story or answer to prayer, be open to someone asking questions or making a comment. Your kids or other family members may then also like to share a miracle or answer to prayer they have experienced.

Model Prayer

> Lord, thank You that You are a prayer-answering God and that You still do miracles today. Our hearts are stirred with faith when we remember all the great and mighty things You have done for us. We ask You now to give us many more amazing stories to tell. And also, God, we ask You to give our children many awesome God-stories that they can pass on to their children and their children's children.

DAY 5

DECISION MAKING

If any of you lacks wisdom, you should ask God, who gives generously to all without finding fault, and it will be given to you (James 1:5 NIV).

S ome decisions are easy to make, like choosing between eggs or cereal. Some seem overwhelming, like choosing which college to attend or whether or not to accept a job offer. No matter the decision, God is there to guide you.

As you pray for wisdom, remember that God's answer can come in a variety of ways: through His Word, an inspired thought, a parent or counselor's wise instruction, an anointed sermon, a worship song, or a friend. A good indicator of the right decision is peace. We read in Colossians 3:15 (AMPC) to let God's peace act as an umpire in our hearts, leading us in the way we should go. If you feel any anxiety or confusion, continue to wait on the Lord, stay in His Word, and ask Him for direction.

Instructions

Ask family members where they need God's help in making a decision. Write down the requests in your prayer journal. Then pray for each person to hear God and receive the direction he or she needs to make the best decision. Be sure to record the answers to serve as a reminder of God's faithfulness.

Model Prayer

Dear Lord, thank You for Your promise that if any one of us lacks wisdom, we can ask and You will give generously. That is just what _____ needs right now. Help _____ to listen for Your voice and faithfully look for Your answer. Help _____ to trust in You and be free from worry and anxiety. Flood _____'s heart with peace to step through the door that You have opened so _____ can clearly know they are walking in Your perfect will.

Day 6

Praying for Your Children's Schools

Jesus said, "Let the little children come to me, and do not hinder them, for the kingdom of heaven belongs to such as these" (Matthew 19:14 NIV).

The hallways of a school can be filled with laughter and friendship, the fields full of cheering parents, and the auditorium full of community participation. However, schools also can be places of stress, bullying, pressure, and loneliness. A positive school environment can change someone's life. For many, the encouragement they receive at school is their only support. Praying over a school not only changes the atmosphere but may even save lives. A healthy school impacts an entire community.

Instructions

Consider prayer walking around your children's school or pray from your car when you are dropping them off or picking them up at school. If you do not have children in school, you may choose to pray for your grandchild's school or a school in your neighborhood. Pray for students, teachers, and staff members, praying by name for those you know. Pray over the building and all the families and community members the school represents. Pray for evil to be restrained—anything that would try to infiltrate the school—such as godless ideologies, sexually explicit or perverted curriculum, drugs, suicide, abuse, violence, and bullying. Invite the presence and power of God to fill every classroom and every life.

Model Prayer

God, we dedicate this school to You, for Your purposes—every classroom and hallway, and all the people and activities in it. We invite Your holy presence and power into every corner and every life there. Shine Your light upon this campus and drive out all darkness, spiritual blindness, perversion to truth, and hostility toward You and Your truth. Father God, stop all attempts to use curricula as a way to disciple our young people in humanism, moral relativism, and godless ideologies. Expose all deception and any efforts made in secrecy to influence and corrupt our children. We lift up every student, teacher, and staff member, and ask You to keep them safe. May every family and community member represented by this school come to know, love, and honor You.

Day 7

Praying for Your Family's Finances

"Bring the whole tithe into the storehouse, that there may be food in my house. Test me in this," says the Lord Almighty, "and see if I will not throw open the floodgates of heaven and pour out so much blessing that there will not be room enough to store it" (Malachi 3:10 NIV).

Almost nothing in life gives us more stress, discontentment, or worry than finances. Money affects almost every area of our lives. But have you ever made it a part of your spiritual life? When we are faithful stewards of our financial resources, God promises to partner with us in providing income to supply all our needs. The apostle Paul reminds us, *"My God will meet all your needs according to the riches of his glory in Christ Jesus"* (Phil. 4:19 NIV). One way we give back to Him is through tithing, which is giving a portion of what He has given us back to Him. You can start by investing 10 percent into His Kingdom work. This way you are acknowledging

His faithfulness and establishing a partnership in expanding His Kingdom.

Instructions

Discuss with your children the importance of investing your income into God's Kingdom. Talk about how you allocate your income for expenses. Then evaluate your family budget: Where do you see God's provision? How well does your budget reflect giving? Together, dedicate your finances to the Lord and pray over your specific needs.

Model Prayer

> Father God, thank You for providing for all our needs. We acknowledge that everything we have comes from You. Forgive us where we have mishandled our money and for times we have not used it wisely. Show us better ways to manage Your provision and give us wisdom. Help us to be good stewards of our finances, to save and invest wisely, and to stay out of debt. Gracious Father, right now we have a need for _____ (share specifically) and we ask You for Your provision. Thank You for promising to meet all of our needs according to Your riches in glory. We delight ourselves in You, Lord, knowing You will give us the desires of our hearts. We commit our ways to You, Lord; we trust in You and know You will act on our behalf (see Ps. 37:4 ESV). In Christ Jesus' name we pray. Amen.

Day 8

Your Family's Future and Calling

For David, after he had served the purpose of God in his own generation, fell asleep (Acts 13:36 AMP).

We are all called to act justly and to love mercy and walk humbly with our God (see Mic. 6:8). In addition, each of us also has a specific calling and, at times, specific assignments to fulfill (see Eph. 2:10). You are not in your family, your house, or your neighborhood by accident; God has plans to use you for His purposes! Asking God to reveal your family's calling may open up new doors of opportunity and new people to serve.

Instructions

As a family:

- Ask God why He placed you in your particular house, neighborhood, school, workplace, city, and nation. What people or needs around you might He be calling you to respond to?

- Identify situations in society that break your heart (in schools, government, neighborhood, or nation).

- Ask God to show your family your specific calling and future direction. Write down and share with one another any special words or ideas that come to mind.

Model Prayer

Lord, we thank You for our family; we are uniquely created for Your good purpose. Though we may not understand what that is right now, we ask that You would prepare us for the future You have planned. Jeremiah tells us that the thoughts and plans You have for us are for good and not for evil, to give us hope and a future (see Jer. 29:11). We also pray that each family member individually will fulfill their calling. Use each of our lives to bring Christ to those around us. Make us a reflection of Your life and truth in this broken world. In Jesus' name we pray. Amen.

DAY 9

CLEANSING YOUR HOME FROM EVIL INFLUENCES

Come out from them and be separate, says the Lord. Touch no unclean thing, and I will receive you (2 Corinthians 6:17 NIV).

After you've dedicated your home to the Lord, you may become more aware of things in your household that displease Him. Are there any belongings there that you know would grieve His Holy Spirit, or that might create an open invitation to any evil forces? Think about the books and movies on your shelves, or posters on the walls of your children's rooms. Consider the music playing in your home or vehicle and on your devices—iPods/phones, computers, etc. How about pictures, magazines, collectibles, and objects used in occult activities, such as Tarot cards, Ouija boards, or astrology charts? Are you aware of how computer or video games in your home are influencing your children?

Like Josiah, king of Israel, when he discovered that pagan idols and worship had crept in and overtaken his kingdom, he repented

225

and cleansed the land of all that displeased the Lord (see 2 Kings 23:1-26). We need to guard over what comes into our homes, including what our children's friends may bring.

This can be a sensitive topic and one in which you will want to ask the Holy Spirit for guidance. Your family may not see these dangers from your perspective and may need God's conviction to come upon their hearts. Older children and teenagers should be encouraged to seek the Lord personally about their belongings and discern what good or evil may be influencing them from their phones and computers.

Note: Bitdefender, a security technology company, has reported children under the age of 10 now account for 10 percent of all visitors to porn video sites, including mega sites like Pornhub. According to Google Analytics, pornography searches increase by 4,700 percent when children are out of school. Tragically, only 3 percent of teenage boys and 17 percent of girls have never seen online pornography.[2] This is a radical problem that is going to require a radical change of heart—a God solution.

As a parent, it's important for you to decide how to keep this out of your home and your children's lives. You may want to discuss with your children their use of the internet and the dangers of accessing inappropriate material. You also may need to apply a digital security solution such as NetNanny or another parental control app. God's Holy Spirit is the best security that can be applied to this problem. When the Holy Spirit comes, He shows us the truth about sin and God's justice and judgment (see John 16:8).

Instructions

Go through your house, room by room, as a family. Ask God to show you, by His Holy Spirit prompting your heart, if there is anything there that He is not pleased with in your home. Also, ask Him to point out to you if any activities are displeasing to Him that He would want you to discontinue. Allow the Lord to give you wisdom and guide you in spiritually cleansing your home.

Model Prayer

Most Holy God, show us anything in our home that is displeasing to You, or dishonors or misrepresents You. Lord, we desire our lives and home to become a place that invites and hosts Your presence. Give us wisdom in cleansing our home from all unholy objects, activities, or influences. We commit to removing and destroying these things, therefore closing the door to the evil one. We declare that our home is dedicated to You, Lord. We welcome You here and thank You for Your love, provision, and protection, in Jesus' name. Amen.

Day 10

Celebrating Communion as a Family

The Lord Jesus, on the night he was betrayed, took bread, and when he had given thanks, he broke it and said, "This is my body, which is for you; do this in remembrance of me." In the same way, after supper he took the cup, saying, "This cup is the new covenant in my blood; do this, whenever you drink it, in remembrance of me" (1 Corinthians 11:23-25 NIV).

When we gather to pray as a family we enter into the very presence of God. The Creator of all Heaven and earth is a great and holy God, yet He freely gives us access to Himself, just as a loving father does to his children (see 1 John 3:1). This is all because of Jesus, who died and rose again *"to make us right with God"* (Rom. 4:25 NLT).

Communion is a time to enjoy our relationship with Christ and remember with thanksgiving all Jesus did for us on the cross. The bread represents how Christ's body was broken so we could be restored and made whole. When we eat the bread, we are proclaiming Jesus' life that now lives within us. When we drink the cup, we celebrate the sacrifice of the Lamb of God and His blood shed for our forgiveness of sins. When we drink, we declare that we are forgiven and washed clean. We are now pure and holy before our Creator and can go boldly into His presence! We did not deserve this priceless and loving sacrifice, but with joy in celebrating communion we honor our heavenly Father for giving us His one and only Son to die for us that we may have a relationship with Him.

Instructions

Gather as a family around the dinner table with a small amount of grape juice (or wine) and some bread or crackers. Begin with some time of confession, asking God to forgive you where you have displeased Him in your life. This can be done individually or shared together as a family. There may even be a need to ask someone there for forgiveness. Then pray this prayer of repentance:

> Lord Jesus, thank You for going to the cross and paying the ultimate sacrifice for my sins. I confess that I have sinned against You through my thoughts, unkind words, and doing things that displease You. I have not loved You with my whole heart; I have not loved others as I love myself. Merciful God, I ask for Your compassion and forgiveness.

Before you receive communion, have someone read 1 Corinthians 11:23-26 over the communion elements. Then, as you partake of the bread, repeat, "This is Christ's body broken for you," and as you drink the juice or wine, "This is Christ's blood shed for you."

Model Prayer

Lord Jesus, it is a privilege for our family to come into Your presence and celebrate communion in remembrance of Your sacrifice. Thank You for dying for us on the cross and paying the price for our sins so that we may be forgiven and receive Your life. Help us to always remember Your sacrifice of love and to walk in thanksgiving for Your precious gift. Amen.

CREATIVE IDEAS
FOR FAMILY PRAYER

A SAMPLE FAMILY ALTAR: TIME
OF PRAYER AND WORSHIP

My house shall be called a house of prayer (Matthew 21:13 ESV).

If you are just getting started with family prayer or looking for a simple plan to get started again, try this model: "Praise, Read, Sing, Pray." This template is especially helpful if you have small children or when your time is limited.

Set aside 15 minutes. Gather your family in the morning or at the end of your day and try using this short, easy-to-follow example:

Praise: Ask your family members to share what God has done for them this day or week. Start by thanking Him. Count your blessings. Praise Him for His goodness and faithfulness toward you and your family. We are encouraged not to forget God's blessings (see Ps. 103:2).

Read Scripture: Read a passage of Scripture (see Ps. 119:105; Matt. 4:4). One dad of little children says he focuses on a few verses, sometimes just one. One night he read Psalm 37, stopping on the final verse: *"because they take refuge in him"* (Ps. 37:40 NIV). He asked, "What does it mean to take refuge in God?" This led to a brief discussion about how when we are afraid, we can run to God with our fears and trust in Him to take care of us.

Sing: After a brief Scripture, this dad suggests two to three songs. If the kids are especially wiggly, it may be only one song! Don't worry if everyone sings either too loudly, softly, or off key. The words of the songs will work deeply in the hearts of everyone (see Ps. 71:23). *"Sing a new song to the Lord, for he has done wonderful deeds. His right hand has won a mighty victory; his holy arm has shown his saving power!"* (Ps. 98:1 NLT).

Pray: After a few songs, pray together. Children can pray a couple short prayers about what's on their heart. You can prompt children to pray for their friends, teachers, the country, or something in the news. Then parents or grandparents can wrap their arms around their children and pray.

- Ask God for their safety, health, success (see Ps. 91:1-16).

- Ask God to give them a good night's sleep (see Prov. 3:24; Ps. 4:8).

- Ask the Lord to make Himself known and to help them walk closely with Him throughout their lives (see John 14:6; James 4:8).

If you are a couple or family without young children and have more time, you may want to refer to the "10-Day Family Prayer Guide" and the "Scriptural Prayers for Your Family" section in the Appendix for other creative ideas.

What if things don't go according to plan? You miss a night? The kids can't sit still? You and your spouse are too exhausted? For sure this will happen! Just start back up as soon as you can. This is too important to give up. The simple plan of "Praise, Read, Sing, and Pray" will help you get back on track.

Model Prayer

Lord, You alone are worthy of our worship! Thank You for giving us a loving family and the privilege of coming together to meet with You. We rejoice in this time together in Your presence—for in Your presence is fullness of joy! Help us as a family to enjoy this intimacy with You regularly. Guide and inspire us to draw near to You and to worship You in fresh ways that will last a lifetime. Amen.

WRITING A FAMILY COVENANT

*Put on then, as God's chosen ones, holy and beloved,
compassionate hearts, kindness, humility, meekness,
and patience, bearing with one another and, if one
has a complaint against another, forgiving each other;
as the Lord has forgiven you, so you also must forgive.
And above all these put on love, which binds everything
together in perfect harmony. And let the peace of Christ
rule in your hearts, to which indeed you were called in
one body. And be thankful. Let the word of Christ dwell
in you richly, teaching and admonishing one another
in all wisdom, singing psalms and hymns and spiritual
songs, with thankfulness in your hearts to God. And
whatever you do, in word or deed, do everything in the
name of the Lord Jesus, giving thanks to God the Father
through him* (Colossians 3:12-17 ESV).

Location

In your family room or at the kitchen table.

Materials Needed

Copies of the Scripture Colossians 3:12-17, pen and paper, large
construction paper, other art supplies if desired, and the sample
family covenant (see below).

Background

A family covenant is a commitment to each other in how you
desire to live and relate to one another. The family covenant appeals
to the heart (a conscious knowledge of right and wrong) rather than
a list of household demands or rules. Our family covenant, like our

covenant with Christ, is not of written laws, but of the Spirit that brings life (see 2 Cor. 3:6 NLT). A family covenant is designed and written by the whole family, both parents and their children, and then signed willingly by everyone. Consider posting it in a high-traffic area in the home as a reminder and point of reference.

Instructions

Read Colossians 3:12-17 aloud, which beautifully lays out godly family values. Discuss with your family the specific values they would like to see exhibited in your home. Take your time and break down the Colossians passage. Give everyone time to add to the conversation their understanding and importance of these biblical principles. To help with this, you also may like to read aloud Matthew 22:37,39 (NIV): *"You shall love the Lord your God with all your heart, and with all your soul, and with all your mind...You shall love your neighbor as yourself"* and Micah 6:8 (ESV): *"to do justice, and to love kindness, and to walk humbly with your God."*

It may help to ask a couple questions: What values would you like our family to be known for? What do you want your friends and neighbors to say about you and our family? Ask each family member to share or write down these desires and character qualities and incorporate them into your family covenant.

If you have children too young to write, Mom or Dad or an older brother or sister can write down their thoughts for them.

On a large piece of construction paper or whiteboard, combine everyone's values into one document to create your family covenant. Talk about these goals and how your family can make them more a part of its lifestyle. Your family covenant can declare your family's intent to mark their lives by these traits. When you have finished writing your family covenant, allow everyone to sign it. If you have time, decorate the covenant and frame it.

Have each person in the family choose one item to pray about. Go around the circle in your prayer time and ask God to help your family live in such a way that this statement is what others would say about your family.

Decide where you will display the family covenant in your home. Some families like to review their covenant once a week, others once a month or several times a year, and then recommit to its values.

Sample Family Covenant

Consider this sample family covenant to inspire your thoughts, but feel free to create your own unique version:

> Our family holds these values dear: kindness, patience, and forgiving one another. We enjoy laughing together, spending time together, helping others, and praying for one another. We will stand by, support, and celebrate one another in both good and in challenging times.
>
> We want others to say about us that we are a family of integrity, honesty, and generosity.
>
> As a family we commit to this covenant out of our love for God and one another because we want to be faithful followers of Jesus Christ and stay true to His Word.

Model Prayer

> Heavenly Father, we know that You have put each one of us into this family for a purpose. We not only have individual destinies, but we have a destiny and calling as a family. When others look at us, we want them

to say, "This is a family who knows God—who we can trust, who reaches out to help others, who (you fill in the blank). Help us to live by our family covenant, as it exemplifies Your Word. May this commitment transform our lives and the way we relate to one another. Help us rebuild our trust in one another if it has been broken. Empower us to live in such a way that people see there is something extraordinary about our family, and that our specialness comes from You. In Jesus' name. Amen.

PRAYING FOR YOUR NEIGHBORHOOD

Satan, who is the god of this world, has blinded the minds of those who don't believe. They are unable to see the glorious light of the Good News. They don't understand this message about the glory of Christ, who is the exact likeness of God (2 Corinthians 4:4 NLT).

Location

Your home and/or around your neighborhood.

Background

Wouldn't it be great if your neighbors came to you and asked you to share with them how they can have peace and hope through Jesus Christ? Just imagine a community where unbelievers have not only the opportunity but the desire to be saved, an environment where people become aware of God's existence, power, and love and want to know Him. This is a community where Christians talk to God about their neighbors before talking to their neighbors about God. They ask the Holy Spirit to cultivate a readiness to receive the

Gospel, covering and supporting every household with His power and love through prayer. We can call this "prayer evangelism." Why not make your community that place?

Instructions

Draw a sketch of your neighborhood (or print a community map from the internet). Mark house numbers and the names of any neighbors you know. Pray for each household, that their eyes and hearts would be opened to Jesus and the power of His love. Ask God to soften their hearts toward Him (see Ezek. 36:26). Pray for their protection and release from the evil one who seeks to keep them in spiritual darkness, separated from God.

To take it a step further, get out for "prayer walks" in your neighborhood. As you pass each house, ask the Holy Spirit to impress on your mind and heart any needs in that household for which you can be praying. Sometimes you can see clues with your physical eyes. Are there children living there? Is the home well cared for or neglected? Are the people at home often or rarely? Observe with your physical sight as well as with spiritual insight. Use what you see and sense to fuel your family's prayers for your neighbors to know Jesus and to feel God's love, presence, and provision in their lives.

Model Prayer

Gracious Lord, we lift up our neighbors to You—some may know You; others may not. But we ask, Lord, that You would show Yourself to all of them. Let them feel Your love and presence and, if they don't know You, give them faith to see You, to reach out to You, and receive Your salvation. Remove the spiritual blindness that keeps them from seeing and embracing You. And give us opportunities to show them Your love and tell them the Good News about Jesus. We pray they respond with faith to become a part of Your eternal family and Your Kingdom! Amen.

PRINCIPLES OF PRAYING TOGETHER

TIPS FOR LEADING A SMALL-GROUP PRAYER MEETING

When praying with your family, it's good to have a simple plan, keeping in mind that family prayer times are more informal and free flowing. As your prayer altar grows, it helps to be more organized and prepared so that everyone stays united and focused. The following suggestions will help you prepare to lead a small-group prayer meeting with extended family, friends, or neighbors in your home.

1. Identify a leader and a mission. Every prayer meeting needs a leader. Otherwise, you will have a number of people trying to lead, and no one knowing exactly who is in charge. This doesn't mean that the leader controls the prayer time, but that they simply facilitate the meeting, make sure it runs smoothly, and listen to the Holy Spirit's direction. Additionally, every

prayer meeting needs a defined purpose or mission. It may be to pray for one another's personal needs or it may be to pray for the needs of your church, community, or school. Without a stated purpose, the prayers can be disjointed, and the prayer time will lack unity, agreement, and focus.

2. Prepare. Effective prayer meetings do not happen by human ingenuity; the Holy Spirit draws people to a place of prayer when He is invited.

    a. Prepare spiritually. You will want to seek the Father's heart for the meeting and pray for the group participants. Pray that the Spirit of prayer would permeate all who participate. *"Now the Lord is the Spirit, and where the Spirit of the Lord is, there is freedom"* (2 Cor. 3:17 NIV).

    b. Prepare the room. Make sure the room is set up beforehand. Do what you can to make the place in which you pray conducive to an unhindered encounter with God. It should be quiet, comfortable, and free of distractions. Pray through the room in advance and over the chairs where people will sit, asking God to anoint the people for powerful prayer.

    c. Prepare resources. Gather prayer requests and praise reports as early as possible, prepare Scriptures, and plan the prayer agenda as the Holy Spirit directs. Prayerfully decide how to communicate the mission of the prayer meeting.

You may want to prepare a brief outline of your prayer group's purpose, agenda, and guidelines for participants.

3. Begin on time. Whether you are beginning with a meal, fellowship, or jumping right into prayer, start on time. Waiting for people to arrive only encourages lateness and discourages "ready-to-go" pray-ers. Your invitation might say something like, "We'll gather at 7 p.m. and begin at 7:15."

4. Set a unified tone for the prayer meeting. Explain the group's mission, plan, and how the meeting will flow. Since people will be at different levels of maturity and understanding about prayer, you can offer guidelines for participating so everyone is "on the same page." Distribute a simple handout of who will lead, how the meeting will run, and how everyone can participate. Newcomers can easily be briefed by providing them with the same information.

5. Establish a prayer mindset. Many prayer groups spend the first 45 minutes talking about their prayer requests, and only the last 15 minutes in actual prayer. You may want to plan for a short time of fellowship, but emphasize that the primary purpose of the prayer meeting is to pray. While your time together may also include a meal, or a brief teaching, it's essential to guard the designated prayer time, especially if you want the serious pray-ers to return.

6. Listen for and share God's direction. As the leader, you must stay open to the Holy Spirit's direction so that you can gently steer the meeting. When I'm leading a small group, I often ask for input from others in the group as we listen to the Holy Spirit together.

7. Incorporate ways for everyone to get involved. Praying in one accord doesn't mean people always pray the same way. Utilize different people's strengths by implementing ways to get everyone to participate. Be gracious but firm in directing the group so that no one person dominates. A good rule of thumb is that the larger the group, the shorter the prayers of each person should be. Give some boundaries to the length of time prayers should be. Try to draw everyone into the time of prayer. If one person is especially shy or quiet (but you know this person is comfortable praying out loud), you may want to ask them to pray over a specific request. Encourage people to pray Scripture. This will help keep prayers focused and in line with God's will.

8. Keep the group on track. The prayer group leader must encourage everyone to pray thoroughly over one request before moving to another one. Allow time for everyone to pray who has something to contribute to that topic. If someone jumps to a new request prematurely, gently bring the group back to the unfinished topic. Usually, a short season of silence

will alert you that prayer for that subject has finished and it's time to move on.

9. Model and encourage faith-filled prayers. Encourage your group to expect great things of God! As you focus on His love and faithfulness rather than the problem, everyone's faith will grow. Pray to Him with an expectation of a miraculous answer! Hebrews 11:6 tells us, *"without faith it is impossible to please God, because anyone who comes to him must believe that he exists and that he rewards those who earnestly seek him"* (NIV).

10. Close on time, on a positive note. To be sensitive to people with other commitments, end the prayer meeting on time. Ending on a positive note is essential so that people look forward to the next prayer time. This can be done with a song, prayer, or hearty amen. If the group is experiencing a special move of God that would warrant extending the meeting, stop at the appointed time and release all those who need to leave before continuing.

OVERCOMING THE OBSTACLES

Unity is a crucial principle for powerful prayer meetings. This guide will help you, as a group leader, to be prepared to handle disruptions so that the meeting will flow smoothly and your prayers will go forward uninterrupted. As a participant in a group, this guide will help you move in united fervent prayer with others.

Being a Ball Hog

In sports, a "ball hog" gets the ball and won't let go. He will try to take the ball and run, dribble, or shoot while everyone else is watching. A team spirit is hindered, which diminishes the team's likelihood of winning. The same is true with prayer. One who hogs the ball—dominates the prayer time—is not a team player.

Sometimes a person who likes to pray the most, and may even be a great pray-er, can become the ball hog! Still, when everyone learns to pray as a team, there will be a new level of God-driven energy and power. As the leader, one way you can redirect the ball hog is to specifically ask different members to pray over particular items, or to remind people at the start of the meeting to limit their praying time to allow everyone the opportunity to pray. You may also need to have a discreet conversation with the offender after the meeting.

Bringing a Personal Prayer Agenda

All needs are genuine, but remember that the Holy Spirit may want something else to transpire. Discernment is critical here. Though the Lord may be speaking to someone to pray about something as an individual, it may not be what He wants the group to pray about in this particular meeting. If someone's personal or emotional burden continues to weigh heavily, you can ask the person if they would like others to pray with them after the meeting concludes. Or ask the person if they feel okay if the meeting moves forward so as to cover other topics.

Praying "Around the World"

This kind of praying goes like this: Someone starts praying for Israel, and the Spirit of the Lord starts bubbling up in you and giving you prayers to pray over Israel. But before you can pray, someone begins to pray for China! You begin to sense what God would have you pray for China, but before you can get a word in edgewise, someone else has started praying for Iraq! Around-the-world prayers kill the momentum of the group. Continue to remind your group to pray for one subject at a time. You may need to stop and gently instruct the group to finish a topic before moving on to another. *"My dear brothers and sisters, take note of this: Everyone should be quick to listen, slow to speak, and slow to become angry"* (James 1:19 NIV).

Rushing into the Throne Room

Some in your group may want to jump in immediately with petitions and declarations before an appropriate period of worship and heart preparation. As the prayer leader, you may need to model a suitable format. You can also ask some of your experienced intercessors to offer opening prayers of adoration, thanksgiving, and confession. You'll find that in some prayer meetings, the Lord may direct more time in worship or repentance than at other times. Each meeting will be unique, but it's up to the leader to be sensitive to the Spirit and guide the meeting accordingly. Always enter in with thanksgiving and praise (see Ps. 100:1-5).

Lack of Eternal Perspective

Your group needs a vision and a focus—a redemptive purpose. Ask, "What is God doing in the big picture? What are the redemptive purposes in our praying today? Why are we praying this way?" Instill in your group that they are there to change the world through their prayers—that nothing is impossible with God!

SCRIPTURAL PRAYERS FOR YOUR FAMILY

PRAYING GOD'S PRAYER PROMISES

Begin your time in prayer by declaring God's promises. These Scriptures promise you that your Heavenly Father does hear your prayers and He will answer them. As you read these promises, your confidence and faith will increase. God declares to us that *"faith comes by hearing, and hearing by the word of God"* (Rom. 10:17 NKJV). We read in Proverbs that the power of life and death are in the tongue (see Prov. 18:21). These Scriptures (all taken from the New King James Version) are life to us and for all those for whom we are praying.

> *I am ready to perform My word* (Jeremiah 1:12).
>
> *Forever, O Lord, Your word is settled in heaven. Your faithfulness endures to all generations; You established the earth, and it abides* (Psalm 119:89-90).

Ask, and you will receive, that your joy may be full (John 16:24).

And whatever things you ask in prayer, believing, you will receive (Matthew 21:22).

Call to Me, and I will answer you, and show you great and mighty things (Jeremiah 33:3).

If you ask anything in My name, I will do it (John 14:14).

Whatever you ask the Father in My name He will give you (John 16:23).

The effective, fervent prayer of a righteous man avails much (James 5:16).

You will make your prayer to Him, He will hear you (Job 22:27).

Now this is the confidence that we have in Him, that if we ask anything according to His will, He hears us (1 John 5:14).

And if we know that He hears us, whatever we ask, we know that we have the petitions that we have asked of Him (1 John 5:15).

And whatever you ask in My name, that I will do, that the Father may be glorified in the Son (John 14:13).

If you abide in Me, and My words abide in you, you will ask what you desire, and it shall be done for you (John 15:7).

So shall My word be that goes forth from My mouth; it shall not return to Me void, but it shall accomplish what I please, and it shall prosper in the thing for which I sent it (Isaiah 55:11).

Assuredly, I say to you, whatever you bind on earth will be bound in heaven, and whatever you loose on earth will be loosed in heaven (Matthew 18:18).

Again I say to you that if two of you agree on earth concerning anything that they ask, it will be done for them by My Father in heaven (Matthew 18:19).

You did not choose Me, but I chose you and appointed you that you should go and bear fruit, and that your fruit should remain, that whatever you ask the Father in My name He may give you (John 15:16).

Then you will call upon Me and go and pray to Me, and I will listen to you (Jeremiah 29:12).

It shall come to pass that before they call, I will answer; and while they are speaking, I will hear (Isaiah 65:24).

He shall call upon Me, and I will answer him; I will be with him in trouble; I will deliver him and honor him (Psalm 91:15).

Let my prayer be set before You as incense, the lifting up of my hands as the evening sacrifice (Psalm 141:2).

Remember God's promise that as you *"delight yourself also in the Lord, ...He shall give you the desires of your heart. ...The steps of a good man are ordered by the Lord, and He delights in his* [your] *way"* (Ps. 37:4,23 NKJV).

PRAYING GOD'S PROMISES
FOR MY CHILDREN

God's Word is full of promises for the children and grandchildren of those who love God. Declare these Scriptures out loud as you make them personal:

> This is what the Lord says: "Restrain your voice from weeping and your eyes from tears, for your work will be rewarded," declares the Lord. "They [your children] will return from the land of the enemy. So there is hope for your descendants," declares the Lord (Jeremiah 31:16-17 NIV).

> The offspring of the righteous will be delivered (Proverbs 11:21 ESV).

> And all your [spiritual] children shall be disciples [taught by the Lord and obedient to His will], and great shall be the peace and undisturbed composure of your children (Isaiah 54:13 AMPC).

> Blessed are those who fear the Lord, who find great delight in his commands. Their children will be mighty in the land; the generation of the upright will be blessed (Psalm 112:1-2 NIV).

> For I will pour water on the thirsty land, and streams on the dry ground; I will pour out my Spirit on your offspring, and my blessing on your descendants (Isaiah 44:3 NIV).

> For thus says the Lord: "Even the captives of the mighty shall be taken, and the prey of the tyrant be rescued, for

I will contend with those who contend with you, and I will save your children" (Isaiah 49:25 ESV).

I keep asking that the God of our Lord Jesus Christ, the glorious Father, may give you the Spirit of wisdom and revelation, so that you may know him better. I pray that the eyes of your heart may be enlightened in order that you may know the hope to which he has called you, the riches of his glorious inheritance in his holy people, and his incomparably great power for us who believe (Ephesians 1:17-19 NIV).

I will contend with him who contends with you, and I will give safety to your children and ease them (Isaiah 49:25 AMPC).

My words which I have put in your mouth shall not depart out of your mouth, or out of the mouth of your [true, spiritual] children, or out of the mouths of your children's children, says the Lord (Isaiah 59:21 AMPC).

PRAYING GOD'S BLESSINGS FOR MY SPOUSE

The best time to pray for your spouse is *every time* you remember to pray for your spouse. For some, morning prayers for your spouse are the best way to begin your coffee routine, because in the flurry of life, it is easy to forget that you have the most power to influence their day on the earth.

You are the closest person to your spouse. On the positive side, you are the one who knows their biggest wins, and on the negative side, you also understand their failures and most inhibiting weaknesses. You see all of it. They are special to you and your family, and your prayers can help them be their best. Morning prayers for your spouse are a fabulous place to start.

Your marriage means you have a front seat to their spiritual life as well and have the opportunity to invest time, energy, and even finances into that intimate and personal part of their life. Yet so often it is easy to forget that the prayers for your spouse will be best aimed coming from you. Do you know how powerful your prayers are for your spouse?

Did you know that your investment in prayer for your spouse will *never* return void? (See Isaiah 55:11.)

So, let's get started!

A Morning Prayer for My Husband

A Morning Prayer for His Day

Dear Lord, I lift my husband's day before you. I pray he senses Your presence today in a strong and mighty way.

Holy Spirit, guide his hands and eyes in all the right places. God, may he find his identity in You first and foremost, enjoy others, and not strive for their respect or their admiration, but I pray others would see his steadfast heart and honor him nonetheless.

Give him favor at work, with his family, with me, and most of all may he find favor with You. Finally, I pray that all of his words and actions today will please You, Lord.

A Morning Prayer for Safety

God, may he leave and come home to us safely, that no evil would befall him.

A Morning Prayer for Blessing

Lord, I bless my husband with wisdom, knowledge, and understanding in every decision he will make today. I bless him with a faithful heart as my husband and with the ability to be a loving, caring, involved father to our kids. Lastly, thank You for giving my husband Your favor and influence to sit among the elders of the gates of our city (see Prov. 31:23).

A Morning Prayer for My Attitude Toward Him

Heavenly Father, give me eyes to see the best in my husband when he walks in the door tonight. In fact, I pray I would see his weariness and know how to comfort and encourage him. Lord, give me the discernment to know how to serve him in Your love.

A Morning Prayer for Wisdom at Work

Oh Lord, please open Your doors of favor to him and give him the wisdom he needs as he steps into every new opportunity. Let him feel Your presence spurring him on as he focuses on his work.

Lastly, I pray for an extra measure of wisdom, and that he would feel the guidance of Your Holy Spirit throughout the day.

In Jesus' name. Amen.

A Morning Prayer for My Wife

A Morning Prayer for Her Day

Heavenly Father, this morning I ask You to bless my wife. Pour Your loving Spirit afresh into her so that Your life will overflow to everyone around her today. Smile on my wife with favor and be gracious to her. Guide her today, give her Your peace, and cause her steps to be directed by Your Holy Spirit.

A Daily Prayer for Strength and Safety

Lord, strengthen my wife and keep her safe; cover her with Your wings and surround her with Your shield of protection. Give her the grace to cast all her cares and concerns on You—that she will walk in Your peace and not be shaken (see Ps. 55:22).

A Morning Prayer for Blessing

Father, give my wife the desires of her heart and make all her plans succeed (see Ps. 20:4). Show my wife Your loving kindness and gracious mercy. Bless her with Your loving presence and shine Your face upon her. Dear Lord, reveal the beauty of Your love through my wife and fill her with the fullness of Your Holy Spirit and power.

A Morning Prayer for Wisdom

Lord, fill my wife with Your understanding and godly wisdom that comes from above. Your wisdom is peace loving, considerate, full of mercy, and bears good fruit. Give her the discernment to know what's best and pure and blameless. And fill her with fruitfulness as she walks before You in righteousness (see Phil. 1:9-11).

Father God, increase her steadfast trust in You. Fill her with knowledge and insight into Your Word. Make her heart strong and true to You.

A Morning Prayer for Peace, Joy, and Love

God of Peace, give my wife Your peace that passes all understanding at all times and in every circumstance. Fill her with exceeding joy. Cause her to abound more and more in Your love. Make her strong in You, so she can do all that You have called her to accomplish (see Phil. 4:7).

I pray especially today that she will know how much both You and I love her.

In Jesus' name. Amen

PRAYING BREAKTHROUGH FOR A TROUBLED MARRIAGE

Pray this for your own marriage or adapt it for the marriage of a family member or friend.

He heals the brokenhearted and binds up their wounds (Psalm 147:3 ESV).

He sent out his word and healed them and delivered them from their destruction (Psalm 107:20).

Based on God's promise in these Scriptures, we now agree as a couple for the total healing, reconciliation, and restoration of our marriage. We agree with Your Word that what God has joined together no person will separate (see Mark 10:9 ESV).

We bless our marriage and pray Your highest and best for our lives and family. Today, may we both know how much You love us and ask that You place that love inside us for one another. We ask You to draw us closer to You and each other. Breathe life and healing into our marriage.

A Prayer of Love

We ask that You would give us the strength and compassion to extend to each other the love, forgiveness, and mercy talked about in 1 Corinthians 13: *"Love is patient, love is kind. It does not envy, it does not boast, it is not proud. It does not dishonor others, it is not self-seeking, it is not easily angered, it keeps no record of wrongs. Love does not delight in evil but rejoices with the truth. It always protects, always trusts, always hopes, always perseveres. Love never fails"* (1 Cor. 13:4-8 NIV).

A Prayer for Strength and Direction

We ask for Your wisdom and strength to know how to handle every situation that we may encounter in our marriage. We pray for Your Holy Spirit's power to be active and alive in us, that we would hear Your voice clearly, and that You would guide us in every decision that we make (see Ps. 55:22).

Healing in Challenging Times

Lord, we turn to You with all our hearts in this challenging and painful time. Heal us spirit, soul, mind, and body. Sustain us during this trying time and help us to choose words and actions that bring life rather than loss or pain.

Discernment and Courage

God of Truth, give each of us the grace to see the ways we have contributed to the problems in our marriage. Help us to be willing to allow You to make the needed changes. Give each of us the courage to take the first step toward forgiveness and reconciliation.

Breaking Free of Strongholds

We break the strongholds from (name things, such as loss, abandonment, addiction, and anger) that the enemy has had over our lives. We let go of bitter roots and judgments, and we ask You to soften our hearts toward You and each other.

Pray Where Appropriate

Gracious Father, bring my spouse face to face with You, even as the prodigal son woke up to realize he was going in the wrong direction and returned to his father's house. I stand in the gap and call out to You,

Mighty God, to protect my spouse from the evil one trying to steal, kill, and destroy our lives and marriage (see Luke 15:11-31; John 10:10-11).

I cry out to You, Lord, to give my spouse a tender heart to seek and call upon You. I ask You to open my spouse's heart to desire to restore our marriage and bring healing to our family. I pray that You would guide us to Your highest and best counselors and advisors who can help us break free of unhealthy patterns (see James 1:5; 3:17; Prov. 1:5).

I declare, Jesus, Your power breaks every demonic stronghold that is operating in or around my spouse's life. Jesus, I thank You that Your blood is enough to overcome every attack, assignment, or stronghold that the enemy has over our marriage. Because of Your work on the cross, I can boldly decree Your word that no weapon that is formed against my spouse, my marriage, or my family will prosper, and any negative words that have been spoken against us will not come to pass. I now claim total and complete victory and restoration for our marriage.

In Jesus' name, I bind all ungodly influences away from my spouse: spirits of pride, unforgiveness, bitterness, offense and division, spirits of separation, divorce, and adultery. I forbid you to operate in my spouse's life.

Lord, thank You that Your kindness leads to repentance. It is Your love that first extends to us so that we are able to respond with love to You and each other.

This is not the end of the story for our marriage. Your plan is to draw us to You, to bring freedom to both of our hearts, to end the cycle of anger, bitterness, and unforgiveness, and to bring us into agreement with Your plan. I trust You and Your power to bring about breakthrough. You are the God of miracles. I trust you for miracles in our marriage today. In Jesus' name. Amen.

PRAYING FOR LOVED ONES TO KNOW CHRIST

And even if our gospel is veiled, it is veiled to those who are perishing, in whose case the god of this world has blinded the minds of the unbelieving so that they will not see the light of the gospel of the glory of Christ, who is the image of God (2 Corinthians 4:3-4 NASB).

Believe on the Lord Jesus, and you will be saved, along with everyone in your household (Acts 16:31 NIV).

- Pray that the person's heart be prepared, so that it will be "good soil" for the seed (see Mark 4:8).

- Pray that satan would not be able to steal the seeds of truth and that nothing else will be able to destroy those seeds (see Mark 4:15-19).

- Pray that the Word becomes revelation through the lifting of the veil (see 2 Cor. 4:3-4). An excellent Scripture to use in prayer is Ephesians 1:17 (ESV): *"That the God of our Lord Jesus Christ, the*

*Father of glory, may give you the Spirit of wisdom
and of revelation in the knowledge of him."*

- Pray that the root of pride in them be broken
  (see 2 Cor. 10:3-5).

- Pray that the person comes to true repentance:

*God may grant them repentance leading to the knowl-
edge of the truth, and they may come to their senses
and escape from the snare of the devil, having been
held captive by him to do his will* (2 Timothy 2:25-26
NASB; see also 2 Pet. 3:9).

As we pray, we realize that *"though we walk in the
flesh, we do not war according to the flesh, for the weapons of our warfare are not of the flesh, but divinely powerful for the destruction of fortresses. Our prayers are
destroying speculations and every lofty thing raised up
against the knowledge of God, and we are taking every
thought captive to the obedience of Christ"* (2 Corinthians 10:3-5 NASB).

Utilize God's Weapons

- All forms of prayer. Supplication, agreement with
  other Christians, travail, praying in the Spirit,
  binding and loosing—any biblical form of prayer
  (see Eph. 6:18).

- Praise. Always praise God with thanksgiving for
  the salvation of the one(s) you are praying for. He
  is faithful (see Ps. 149:5-9).

- The Word of God. Speaking and praying Scriptures that apply to your situation releases great power against the enemy (see Eph. 6:17).

- The name of Jesus. Praying in the name above every name, Christ Jesus, and in the authority He has given to us, binds demonic powers and strongholds (see Luke 10:17).

In daily prayer, wage spiritual warfare over your loved one.

We are human, but we don't wage war as humans do. We use God's mighty weapons, not worldly weapons, to knock down the strongholds of human reasoning and to destroy false arguments. We destroy every proud obstacle that keeps people from knowing God. We capture their rebellious thoughts and teach them to obey Christ (2 Corinthians 10:3-5 NLT).

Ask your heavenly Father to help you identify the strongholds that influence your loved one's belief system, that hinder them from accepting Jesus. Then, in Jesus name, "bind" these hindrances and forbid them from operating against your loved one. These hindrances may include ungodly or calculative reasoning, human wisdom or logic, or wrong information learned over time that governs their mindset. These ungodly belief systems may consist of philosophies, false religions (humanism, atheism, Hinduism, Buddhism, Islam, racism, intellectualism, Judaism, materialism) and roots of rejection, perversions, alcoholism, and other addictions that cause a person to reject Jesus.

Pray:

> In the name of the Lord Jesus Christ, I am destroying
> you, stronghold of _____.
>
> Father God, I pull down and destroy every lofty thing
> raised up against the knowledge of God in my loved
> one's life (see 2 Cor. 10:5). Lord, I ask You to pull up
> the root of pride (this involves the desire to rule our
> own lives, deciding for ourselves what's righteous or
> unrighteous, and basically becoming our own god).
>
> I take every thought in my loved one's life captive to the
> obedience of Christ (refers to spontaneous thoughts
> and temptations satan uses to assault the unbelievers,
> as well as the schemes and plans he uses to keep them
> in darkness). I ask you, God, to shield my loved one
> from satan's thoughts and temptations.
>
> In the name of the Lord Jesus Christ, I bind all strong-
> holds of _____ that have blinded my loved
> one's eyes, and I call for the true light of God to shine
> upon their heart.

Be encouraged:

> *The Lord is not slow to fulfill his promise as some count
> slowness, but is patient toward you, not wishing that
> any should perish, but that all should reach repentance*
> (2 Peter 3:9 ESV).

Adapted from Dutch Sheets, *How to Pray for Lost Loved Ones*
(Ventura, CA: Regal Books, 2001).

PSALM 91 PRAYER OF PROTECTION FOR MY FAMILY

Personalized from Psalm 91 (TLB)

1. My family and I live within the shadow of the Almighty; sheltered by the God who is above all gods.

2. This I declare, that He (Jehovah God) alone is my family's refuge, our place of safety; He (the Lord Almighty) is our God, and we trust in Him.

3. For He rescues my family and me from every trap and protects us from the fatal plague.

4. He (Almighty God) will shield my family with His wings! They will shelter us. His faithful promises are our armor.

5. Now we don't need to be afraid of the dark anymore, nor fear the dangers of the day.

6. We won't fear the plagues of darkness, nor disasters in the morning.

7. Though a thousand fall at our side, though ten thousand are dying around us, the evil will not touch us.

8. My family will see how the wicked are punished, but we will not share it.

9. For Jehovah is our refuge! We choose the Lord of all Heaven and earth, who is above all gods, to shelter us.

10. How then can evil overtake us or any plague come near?

11. For He orders His angels to protect us wherever we go.

12. They will steady my family and me with their hands to keep us from stumbling against the rocks on our journey.

13. My family and I can safely walk past a lion or destroy poisonous snakes, yes, even trample them beneath our feet!

14. For the Lord says, because my family and I love Him, He will deliver us; God will make my family and me great because we trust in His name.

15. When we call on the Lord, He will answer; He will be with us in trouble, rescue us, and honor us.

16. God will satisfy my family and me with long life and give us His salvation.

Praying for Healing

If two of you shall agree on earth as touching any thing that they shall ask, it shall be done for them of my Father which is in heaven. For where two or three are gathered together in my name, there am I in the midst of them (Matthew 18:19-20 KJV).

Based on God's promise in this Scripture, we now agree with (insert name) _____ for the release of all the things God deems necessary for them to walk in perfect health and healing.

We thank You, Jehovah Rapha (the Lord who heals), that You are miraculously, completely, and totally healing _____ and that they are being restored to full health, strength, mobility, and vitality. We declare, in Jesus' name, the One who bore _____'s grief and sorrows, sins and sicknesses, that by Your stripes they are healed (see Isa. 53:4-5).

Has God not said, *"He gives power to the faint and weary, and to him who has no might He increases strength [causing it to multiply and making it to abound]"* (Isa. 40:29 AMPC)?

We decree, in Jesus' name, that no plague can come near them (see Ps. 91:10). No disease, germ, virus, or destructive bacteria can live in any part of their body—that any disease, germ, virus, or destructive bacteria that tries to thrive in their body is being burned out by the power of the Holy Spirit.

We speak Your word over _____, that *"there is nothing covered that will not be revealed, and hidden that will not be known"* (Matt. 10:26 NKJV). We come together in agreement and in faith that You are uncovering the perfect solution to rid their body of all sickness. We declare that all bacteria and all disease must bow its knee to the name of Jesus—that it cannot defy or resist the Word and the healing power of God.

We thank You, Lord, that You are giving divine wisdom to (insert doctor's name) _____ and that they come into agreement with Your perfect will in how to treat _____.

We thank You that only those things that are good and beneficial will be done to and for _____ and that they will receive Your highest and best medical treatment.

Lord, You told us that this is the confidence we have in approaching You, that if we ask anything according to Your will, You hear us. And if we know that You hear us—whatever we ask—we know that we have what we asked of You. Therefore, with confidence we stand in faith, knowing that You are hearing and answering our prayers, in Jesus' name. Amen (see 1 John 5:14-15).

BIBLICAL PRAYERS FOR SPIRITUAL AWAKENING IN OUR NATION

E ach of these bolded sections is a characteristic or condition of people's lives when they are being prepared for or visited by a move of the Holy Spirit. When you pray these prayers, you are asking God to come and prepare the hearts of His people and to bring those who do not know Him to Christ.

I Pray for God's Mercy upon Our Lives

Based upon Psalm 85:4-7; Lamentations 3:22; Daniel 9:18-19.

Holy Father, I come before You in Jesus' name; I humbly plead for Your mercy upon my life, the Church, and this nation. Lord, help us to understand deeply and with a contrite heart that we deserve Your judgment far more than Your blessing. Our nation has trampled on Your great name; we have all compromised Your Word, but we plead for Your mercy and forgiveness.

I Pray for a Spirit of Brokenness and Repentance
Based upon Psalm 51:7; Proverbs 28:13; 2 Corinthians 7:1,10.

Righteous God, please send by Your Spirit an overwhelming conviction of our sin, of my sin, and give us all a deep and sincere brokenness and genuine repentance, turning us back to You and Your Kingdom purpose. Grant our nation and Your people a true godly sorrow that leads us to turn from our wrongful ways of living. Fill us with holy fear and reverence for Your name. Purify Your Church, purify me, for Your glorious purpose.

I Pray for Boldness, Holiness, and Power in Christian Leaders
Based upon 1 Timothy 3:1-2; 2 Timothy 1:6-7; 1 Corinthians 2:4.

Mighty God, make alive Your Word and Spirit in our leaders with deep repentance, dynamic power, and a renewed passion for You. Transform the hearts and minds of Your Church leaders, giving them a burning passion to seek Your face with holy boldness, and a burning passion to live uncompromisingly.

I Pray for an Intimate Return to You in Fervent Prayer
Based upon Jeremiah 29:13; Psalm 24:3-5; Matthew 5:6; 21:13; James 4:8; 5:16.

Righteous God, give Your Church, give me, a burning hunger for Your presence and a passion for effectual and fervent prayer. Draw us near to You, giving us clean hands and pure hearts. Lord, give us a hunger and thirst for You above all else. Transform the heart of Your Church, transform my family and me, to become a house of prayer for all nations.

I Pray for Unity in the Church and Restored Families

Based upon John 13:34-35; 15:12; 17:20-22; 1 Corinthians 1:10.

Holy Father, please instill unity in Your Church and harmony among Your people. Give us one heart and mind to love You and one another. Help us in humility to tear down the strongholds of disunity and serve together in fulfilling Your Kingdom purpose in this land. Bring a heart of love, forgiveness, and reconciliation to Christian families everywhere, including in my own family. Restore in us a steadfast heart toward You and a strong desire to be a part of building Your Kingdom.

I Pray for Passion for Spreading God's Good News

Based upon John 3:16; Luke 19:10; Acts 1:8; Romans 5:5; 9:1-3; 2 Peter 3:9.

Gracious Lord, fill Your Church, fill me, with a burning passion for those who are lost and dying without Christ. Give us the same singleness of heart and purpose You gave Jesus, for those who do not yet know You.

I Pray for a Passion for Your Mission

Based upon Matthew 18:12; 24:14; 28:19; Luke 19:10; Acts 1:8.

Righteous God, empower Your people, empower me, to burn with passion to fulfill Your Kingdom purpose in the places where You have planted us. Grant to us a fiery zeal to expand Your Kingdom.

I Pray for an Increase in Laborers

Based upon Matthew 9:37-38; Acts 1:8.

Lord of the Harvest, awaken thousands of believers to fulfill Your Kingdom mission and radiate the light and love of Christ. Send forth a flood of laborers into Your harvest field.

I Pray for Pure Motives and Your Kingdom Purpose

Based upon Matthew 6:33; Hebrews 4:12; James 4:1-4.

Holy Lord, we ask You to deepen our understanding and purify our motives for a powerful spiritual awakening. Lord, teach us how to seek Your face and not just Your hand. Cause us to seek You first, not just Your comfort and blessings. Dear God, teach us to pray for Your glory, honor, and praise to fill the land.

I Pray for the Salvation and Wisdom of Government and Social Leaders

Based upon Psalm 2:8; Romans 2:4; 1 Timothy 2:1-4.

Holy Father, I desperately ask for a mighty move of Your convicting presence to fill the halls of government offices. Raise up the spirit of godliness, justice, and truth in every place of cultural influence. We ask You to pour out Your convicting and transforming presence and saving power upon governmental leaders, educators, the media, journalists, and the entertainment and sports industries. We ask that You reveal Your goodness and grace so that millions will be converted to Christ in every community of cultural influence.

I Pray for Sweeping Revival in the Church

Based upon Psalm 80:19; 85:6; Isaiah 57:15; 2 Chronicles 7:14; James 4:8.

Righteous Lord, I ask You to send sweeping revival and awaken Your Church. Whatever it takes to bring Your Church to its knees, prepare the soil of our hearts. Father, we pray not for shallow, selfish ends, but for Your great glory and Kingdom to prevail. Cause us to come to You in true humility, brokenness, and contriteness of heart.

I Pray for Global Spiritual Awakening and Great Harvest

Based upon Isaiah 64:1; Matthew 24:14; 2 Peter 3:9; Revelation 22:17,20.

Sovereign God, we ask You to open the heavens and send forth Your awesome manifest presence. We ask You to reveal Your undeniable goodness and the power of Your salvation to the whole earth, bringing unprecedented multitudes to Your Son, Christ Jesus. We ask You to arise and reveal Yourself even greater than in any previous awakening. Mighty God, I pray for a great harvest of souls in this generation and before the glorious return of Christ Jesus.

SCRIPTURAL PRAYERS FOR EMERGING GENERATIONS

*L*et God arise and the enemies of our children be scattered (see Ps. 68:1)!

The Lord has a great plan for this emerging generation—they will take the Gospel into every sphere of influence and contend for the cultural keys to our nation. At the same time, our enemy is actively at work strategizing how he can destroy our children. Just as he sought to kill Joseph, Moses, and Jesus, he wants to stop this young generation from fulfilling their God-given destinies.

As godly parents and members of Christ's Kingdom, we must both raise up the next generation in God's truth and come alongside them in fervent prayer—to defeat hopelessness, addictions, discouragement, and perversion.

It is time for us to stand with this generation in their life's battles, interceding for the preservation of their destinies.

Contending with Purpose and Destiny

Heavenly Father and Creator of all life, You have dreamed a unique dream for every individual. Therefore, we cry out and say, "The destinies of our children will be preserved!"

Give this emerging generation vision and a sense of purpose regarding their future. Father God, it is time to restore this generation and bring them forth to fulfill Your heart! Raise up sons and daughters with godly purpose and destiny to contend for the future of our nation (see Isa. 22:22). Raise up ones who will lead the way for righteousness and justice in every mountain of cultural influence. May they, like David, fulfill the purpose of God in their generation (see Acts 13:36).

Discerning Life-Giving Relationships

Father God, You said that it is not outward appearances that are important to You, but it's the condition of our hearts. Give our sons and daughters pure hearts. Give them godly discernment in choosing friends. Reveal to them the importance of good character rather than looks or popularity (see 1 Sam. 16:7). Give them godly wisdom and courage to keep away from relationships that would take them down a path of destruction. Bring across their paths life-giving mentors, friendships, and at the right time, the lifelong mate You have chosen for them to walk with and together fulfill their God-given calling.

Finding Freedom

Jesus, You are the great deliverer. In Your name, Lord Jesus, I call out to You to arise and contend against the enemies of our children and bring them Your salvation. I intercede for freedom from a rebellious spirit, freedom from sexual addiction, and freedom from drugs and the occult. We call for a spiritual jailbreak for our own children and the youth of our nation (see Isa. 49:25). Open their eyes to discover the abundant life that comes only through a close and intimate relationship with Jesus Christ (see John 10:10).

Healing Fatherlessness

Abba Father, You said You would be a Father to the fatherless (see Ps. 68:5). I cry out for this emerging generation and ask that You would pour out Your Father's heart and heal them. Deliver our children from a spirit of death and release them into Your abundant life.

Raise up spiritual parents across our nation to love them and guide them in fulfilling their destiny and God-given calling.

Thank You for Your promise to send forth the spirit of Elijah to return the hearts of the fathers to the children and the children to their fathers (see Mal. 4:6). Therefore, I confidently ask, in the name of Jesus Christ, that You will restore and heal broken relationships between fathers and mothers and their sons and daughters.

Raise up a generation of men who will be present, engaged, and faithful. I pray for fathers and mothers to arise who will teach their children Your ways and the reverence of the Lord.

I pray today for You, O God, to release a discipling movement that will bring a fatherless generation into the deep security of sonship and daughtership with You.

Overcoming Hopelessness

In Jesus' mighty name, I cast down all thoughts of suicide, depression, hopelessness, and despair and declare that they are broken off our children's lives. Father God, encourage them today and send someone to let them know how much You love them.

Thank You, Lord, that Your thoughts toward our children are thoughts for good and peace and not of evil, to give them a future and a hope (see Jer. 29:11). Therefore, we pray with expectation and confidence that our children will experience salvation and the joy that comes with knowing You.

Protecting from the Evil One

Mighty God, deliver this emerging generation from evil and all the plans of the enemy who comes to steal, kill, and destroy (see John 10:10). In Jesus' name, I declare that no weapon formed against our children will prosper this day (see Isa. 54:17).

I ask You, the Great Shepherd, to guide the steps of our children out of the path of death and destruction. Put a shield around them to protect them spiritually, physically, mentally, and emotionally. Station Your angels around about them to protect them and keep them in the ways of the Lord (see Ps. 91:11). I lay hold of Your promises for protection and declare that You will always satisfy our children with long life and show them Your salvation (see Ps. 91:16).

Prospering in School

Lord, I pray that You would guide the steps of every child in this generation to the schools where they will best learn and prosper. Bless them with Your highest and best teachers spiritually and academically. Send godly influences to our children who will encourage them in their studies and their walk with Jesus Christ. Protect our children from distractions that would draw them away from You and from the education and career path You have for them.

Give our children and young people the courage to say "no" to negative peer pressure. Protect them from getting involved in gangs, drugs, sex, and other destructive activities that may have infiltrated their schools. May they experience school as a place of safety, security, and personal growth, with good and godly education. Insulate them with Your truth and empower them by Your spirit as they walk in this world.

Releasing a Youth Revival

God of Revival, raise up this young generation to ignite spiritual awakening across our nation, releasing a holy cleansing flood of Your presence that will sweep millions of youth into God's Kingdom (see 1 John 1:7). I declare that healing and deliverance shall break out over the nation and the Shalom of God will fill our sons and daughters (see Isa. 54:13). Lord of the Harvest, pour out Your promised rain of salvation and refreshing upon our sons and daughters (see Joel 2:28). Raise up youth who are not ashamed of the Gospel and who will release the power of Your good news to blaze across the land.

Seven Powerful Life-Giving Prayers for Your Church

1. An atmosphere of "open heavens" that invites God's presence, bringing the fear of the Lord to every service and breaking all hindrances to what God wants to do (see Deut. 28:12). God's supernatural power is both felt and seen.

2. An atmosphere that invites humility, repentance, and forgiveness: *"Who is allowed to ascend the mountain of the Lord? Who may go up to his holy dwelling place? The one whose deeds are blameless and whose motives are pure, who does not lie, or make promises with no intention of keeping them"* (Ps. 24:3-4 NET).

3. An atmosphere conducive to hear and discern the voice of God: sensitivity of leadership and the congregation to hear from the Holy Spirit what God wants us to do and His timing for it (see John 10:27; Heb. 3:7-8).

4. An atmosphere of liberty: displayed in Spirit-empowered proclamation of the Gospel, which lays a foundation of biblical truth, resulting in a great harvest of souls and releasing believers into their God-given callings (see Isa. 61:1-11; Dan. 11:32); an atmosphere of exuberant, joy-filled praise and extraordinary God-honoring worship that breaks off discouragement and oppression (see Ps. 95:1-3).

5. An atmosphere of unified expectancy and faith: people believe that nothing is impossible with God; no problem is too big for Him (see Matt. 19:26).

6. An atmosphere of financial blessing and breakthrough: embracing the belief that God desires to provide for His people and desires to provide for His Kingdom work. People have faith to give generously and reap financial and Kingdom benefits (see 2 Cor. 9:8; Luke 6:38).

7. An atmosphere conducive to vision: inward vision—seeing what God wants to do in the church—and also outward vision—seeing how to pray for and transform the community outside the four walls of the church building (see Matt. 28:19).

NOTES

Chapter 1: The Vision: Lighting the Nation

1. Norman V. Williams, *How to Have a Family Altar*, (Chicago, IL: Moody Press, 1951), 2.

Chapter 2: What Is an Altar?: Why Your Family Needs One

1. Cheryl Sacks, The *Prayer Saturated Family* (Minneapolis, MN: Chosen, a Division of Baker Publishing Group, 2016), 37-38.
2. Ibid., 93.
3. John Mulinde and Mark Daniel, *Prayer Altars* (Orlando, FL: World Trumpet Mission Publishing, 2013), 58.
4. Ibid., 59.

Chapter 3: Why Satan Opposes the Family: It's All-Out War!

1. See Acts 11:14; 16:14,31.
2. Branka Vuleta, "Divorce Rate in America: 35 Stunning Stats for 2022," Blog, Legal Jobs, January 28, 2021, https://legaljobs.io/blog/divorce-rate-in-america.

3. Manny Alvarez, "Porn Addiction: Why Americans are in More Danger Than Ever," Fox News Mental Health, January 16, 2019, https://www.foxnews.com/health/porn -addiction-why-americans-are-in-more-danger-than-ever.

4. NetNanny, "The Detrimental Effects of Pornography on Small Children," December 19, 2017, https://www.netnanny .com/blog/the-detrimental-effects-of-pornography-on -small-children.

5. See Matthew 5:27-28; 19:18; 1 Corinthians 6:9-11.

6. See Genesis 1:27-28.

7. Kyle Morris and Sam Dorman, "Over 63 Million Abortions have Occurred in the US since Roe v. Wade Decision in 1973," Fox News, May 4, 2020.

8. Sean Salai, "U.S. in League with China, North Korea, on Abortion," *The Washington Times,* January 31, 2022.

9. "Child Sexual Abuse Facts," YWCA.org.

10. Kathryn Darden, "Communist Agenda Found in 1958 Book, 1963 Congressional Record," Christian Activities, May 12, 2020, https://www.christianactivities.com/communist -agenda-found-in-1963-congressional-record.

11. Elizabeth Youmans, Jill Thrift, and Scott Allen, *As the Family Goes so Goes the Nation* (Orlando, FL: Chrysalis International, Inc., 2013), 40.

12. Ibid., 4.

13. Dutch Sheets, *Authority in Prayer* (Minneapolis, MN: Bethany House, 1995), 21.

Chapter 4: The Family Can Save the Nation: One Household at a Time

1. Will Ford, "The Prayers of My Forefathers (Former Slaves) Echo Today, 150 Years After the Civil War," willfordministries .com.

2. "Underground Railroad," Quakersintheworld.org.
3. Kaleena Fraga, checked by Jaclyn Anglis, "The Inspiring Story of Corrie Ten Boom, the Dutch Watchmaker Who Saved 800 Jews from the Holocaust," allthatsinteresting.com.
4. Sacks, *The Prayer Saturated Family*, 25-26.
5. William R. Osborne, "A House with Open Doors: Betsie and Corrie Ten Boom," May 11, 2020, https://credomag .com/2020/05/a-house-with-open-doors-betsie-and-corrie -ten-boom.

Chapter 5: How to Spend Time Alone with God: Creating a Place to Encounter Him

1. Arlyn Lawrence and Cheryl Sacks, *Prayer Saturated Kids* (Colorado Springs, CO: NavPress, 2007), 95-96.
2. Keith Wooden, *Teaching Children to Pray* (Grand Rapids, MI: Zondervan, 1992), 27.

Chapter 6: Enriching Your Marriage Through Prayer: More Intimacy, Less Conflict

1. Williams, *How to Have a Family Altar*, 11-12.
2. W. Bradford Wilcox, a sociology professor and director of the National Marriage Project at the University of Virginia, co-authored the research with Christopher Ellison at the University of Texas, San Antonio, and Amy Burdette, Florida State University. They relied on data from the 2006 National Survey of Religion and Family Life of 2,400 adults ages 18 to 59.
3. Sacks, *The Prayer Saturated Family*, 41-42.

Chapter 7: Getting Started with Family Prayer: Ways to Engage Everyone

1. Sacks, *The Prayer Saturated Family*, 111-112.
2. Ibid., 117.

Chapter 8: Blessing Your Children: Imparting Life-Changing Words

1. Jack Zenger and Joseph Folkman, "The Ideal Praise-to-Criticism Ratio," Harvard Business Review, or Debbie Guinn, "How to Give Meaningful Blessings to Children," Ministry Spark.
2. Lawrence and Sacks, *Prayer Saturated Kids*, 49-50.
3. Ibid., 51-52.
4. William T. Ligon, Sr., *Imparting the Blessing to Your Children* (Brunswick: Shalom, Inc, 1989), 17.
5. Ibid., 13.
6. Lawrence and Sacks, *Prayer Saturated Kids,* 58.
7. Ibid., 57-58.
8. Ibid., 58.

Chapter 9: Prayer with the Family of God: Discover Exponential Results When the Ekklesia Stands Together

1. See Matthew 3:11; Luke 3:16.
2. See Acts 1:8; Philippians 4:13.
3. See Matthew 10:7-8; Hebrews 13:7-8.
4. Jim Cymbala, *Fresh Wind, Fresh Fire* (Grand Rapids, MI: Zondervan, 1997), 60-66.
5. Cindy Jacobs, *The Reformation Manifesto: Your Part in God's Plan to Change Nations Today* (Bloomington, MN: Bethany House Publishers, 2008), 44-47.
6. Ibid., 48.
7. "The Time for Prayer: The Third Great Awakening," Christianity Today, Issue 23: "Spiritual Awakenings in North America," 1989, https://www.christianitytoday .com/history/issues/issue-23/time-for-prayer-third-great -awakening.html.

Chapter 10: How to Create a Life-Giving Atmosphere in Your Home: Living Under an Open Heaven

1. Sacks, *The Prayer Saturated Family*, 51.

Chapter 11: Igniting Revival: The Difference Your Prayer Altar Makes

1. Kerby Anderson, "The Decline of a Nation," Probe Ministries, 1991.

2. Gregory A. Smith, "About Three-in-Ten U.S. Adults Are Now Religiously Unaffiliated," Pew Research Center, December 14, 2021.

3. Michael Gryboski, "Only 6 Percent of Americans Have 'Biblical Worldview,' Research from George Barna Finds," The Christian Post, May 26, 2021.

4. Barna, "Changing Worldview Among Christians Over the Past 13 Years," Barna Research Group, March 9, 2009.

5. Barna, "American Worldview Inventory 2022, Release #3: A Detailed Look at How the Worldview of Parents of Preteens Misses the Mark," Arizona Christian University, April 12, 2022.

6. Ibid.

7. Barna, "Are We Losing the Next Generation?" BattleCry, November/December 2010.

8. Mulinde and Daniel, *Prayer Altars*, 29.

9. Chris Vennetti, *Journey into the Spirit Empowered Life* (Orlando, FL: Disciple Nations International, 2014), 171-172.

10. "The Trumpet Call," Ministry videos Godtube.com.

11. Chris Vennetti, *Journey into the Spirit Empowered Life*, 171-172.

12. Mulinde and Daniel, *Prayer Altars*, 13.

13. Ibid., 14-15.

A 10-Day Family Prayer Guide

1. Gary Smalley and John Trent, *The Blessing* (Nashville, TN: Thomas Nelson, 2004), 109.

2. NetNanny, "The Detrimental Effects of Pornography on Small Children," https://www.netnanny.com/blog/the -detrimental-effects-of-pornography-on-small-children.

ABOUT THE AUTHOR

Cheryl Sacks is a best-selling author, national conference speaker, prayer mobilizer, and church prayer consultant. Her *Prayer-Saturated* book series—including *The Prayer Saturated Church, Prayer Saturated Kids*, and *The Prayer Saturated Family*—has blessed and mentored tens of thousands of individuals and families to go deeper into prayer. She has written multiple prayer guides, including *Reclaim a Generation: 21 Days of Prayer for Schools,* available at prayershop.org.

Cheryl's heart is to see families healed, restored, and empowered by the Holy Spirit, to ignite the spiritual awakening and revival fires He wants to bring to their homes and nation. Cheryl and her husband, Hal, are founders and leaders of BridgeBuilders International Leadership Network, a transformational prayer ministry located on the Arizona Christian University campus in the Phoenix, Arizona, ,area. They have a married daughter and three beautiful grandchildren. You can learn more about Cheryl and Hal's ministry at bridgebuilders.net and prayersaturated.life.